Elementary Online Learning

Elementary Online Learning offers school- and district-level leaders and administrators a field-tested approach to developing formal and interdisciplinary online education, in-house and from scratch, for grades K-5. While it is possible today to purchase off-the-shelf online platforms from for-profit companies, many elementary schools have the option of creating their own programs, curricula, and instructional strategies that are deliberately tailored to the strengths and needs of their own communities. This book provides practical and effective approaches to cohesive, data-driven program design, synchronous and asynchronous teaching, professional development, family partnerships, and much more. Each chapter is full of research-based ideas, recommendations, and prompts that will help schools yield online education that is interdisciplinary, socially just, and student-driven.

Lana Peterson is Director of Community Engagement in the Learning + Technologies Collaborative at the University of Minnesota, USA, and holds an elementary education teaching license.

Holly Skadsem is District Digital Learning and Online Elementary School Coordinator at Bloomington Public Schools, USA, a licensed administrator, and a former elementary school teacher.

Also Available from Routledge
Eye On Education
(www.routledge.com/k-12)

The Brain-Based Classroom
Accessing Every Child's Potential Through Educational Neuroscience
Kieran O'Mahony

Thriving as an Online K-12 Educator
Essential Practices from the Field
Edited by Jody Peerless Green

Coding as a Playground
Programming and Computational Thinking in the Early Childhood Classroom
Marina Umaschi Bers

Elementary Online Learning

Strategies and Designs for Building Virtual Education, Grades K-5

Lana Peterson and Holly Skadsem

Routledge
Taylor & Francis Group

NEW YORK AND LONDON

Cover image: © Getty Images

First published 2023
by Routledge
605 Third Avenue, New York, NY 10158

and by Routledge
4 Park Square, Milton Park, Abingdon, Oxon, OX14 4RN

Routledge is an imprint of the Taylor & Francis Group, an informa business

© 2023 Lana Peterson and Holly Skadsem

The right of Lana Peterson and Holly Skadsem to be identified as authors of this work has been asserted in accordance with sections 77 and 78 of the Copyright, Designs and Patents Act 1988.

All rights reserved. No part of this book may be reprinted or reproduced or utilised in any form or by any electronic, mechanical, or other means, now known or hereafter invented, including photocopying and recording, or in any information storage or retrieval system, without permission in writing from the publishers.

Trademark notice: Product or corporate names may be trademarks or registered trademarks, and are used only for identification and explanation without intent to infringe.

Library of Congress Cataloging-in-Publication Data
Names: Peterson, Lana, author. | Skadsem, Holly, author.
Title: Elementary online learning : designing and building virtual education, grades K-5 / Lana Peterson and Holly Skadsem.
Description: New York, NY : Routledge, 2022. | Includes bibliographical references. | Identifiers: LCCN 2022012802 (print) | LCCN 2022012803 (ebook) | ISBN 9781032226415 (hardback) | ISBN 9781032250854 (paperback) | ISBN 9781003281498 (ebook)
Subjects: LCSH: Web-based instruction—Minnesota—Bloomington. | Education, Elementary—Minnesota—Bloomington. | New Code Academy (Bloomington, Minn.)
Classification: LCC LB1028.57 .P47 2022 (print) | LCC LB1028.57 (ebook) | DDC 371.33/44678077657—dc23/eng/20220503
LC record available at https://lccn.loc.gov/2022012802
LC ebook record available at https://lccn.loc.gov/2022012803

ISBN: 978-1-032-22641-5 (hbk)
ISBN: 978-1-032-25085-4 (pbk)
ISBN: 978-1-003-28149-8 (ebk)

DOI: 10.4324/9781003281498

Typeset in Palatino
by Apex CoVantage, LLC

Contents

Preface xi
Acknowledgements xv

1   Introduction 1
    Voices from New Code Academy 3
    Spotlight on Practice: Should We Build a K-12
        Online School by Fall? 3
    The Conception of New Code Academy 5
    Spotlight on Practice: Taking a Leap of Faith to
        Online Teaching 8
    A Day We Will Never Forget 9
    Guiding Instructional Research and Framework 9
    Community of Inquiry 10
    Learning Coach 12
    Cognition and the Brain 12
    Spotlight on Practice: Key Aspects of High-Quality
        Learning Experiences 14
    Culturally Responsive Teaching 15
    Universal Design for Learning 16
    Elementary Learners 17

2   Establishing a Lens of Equity and Social Justice 21
    What is Equity? 22
    Access 22
    Spotlight on Practice: Knowing Learners Culturally,
        Academically, and Personally to Build Equitable
        Instruction. 23
    Achievement 25
    Identity 26

Spotlight on Practice: Sometimes the Best Professional
    Development Includes 'Unlearning'...................28
Power..30

3 Building the Foundation of New Learning............35
Purchasing vs. Building Curriculum 35
School Design Teams....................................36
Spotlight on Practice: Permission and Compassion.......38
Interdisciplinary Curriculum...........................40
Spotlight on Practice: This Is What Teaching
    Is About...44
Spotlight on Practice: Building Interdisciplinary
    Curriculum Provides a High Return on
    Investment 48
Building in Parallel 49

4 Designing an Elementary Online Program.............53
Program Design Development 53
Brain-Based Learning 55
Structure 58
    Schedule 58
    Communication......................................61
Staffing and Leadership 62
Spotlight on Practice: Online Physical Education
    Builds Real-life Fitness and Health................64
Partner School 66
Instructional Staff 66
Leadership Model 68
Partnering and Program Evaluation......................69
Resources 69
Spotlight on Practice: Using Materials to Move
    From Concrete to Abstract Online 71
Technology 73
Food...74

5	**Facilitating Teacher Professional Development**........77
	Spotlight on Practice: Embrace the Change
	of Teaching Online....................................78
	Back to School Professional Development...............79
	Instructional Coaching 81
	Spotlight on Practice: Doing More by Doing Less,
	an Exercise in Glass and Rubber Balls 83
	End of the Year Reflective Focus Groups................86
	Spotlight on Practice: Misconceptions About
	Online Learning......................................89
	Curriculum and Lesson Documentation 91

6	**Launching the First 20 Days Online** 95
	Planning the First 20 Days 96
	Digital Competencies 98
	Routines and Rituals..................................98
	Community Building 99
	Spotlight on Practice: Breaking Down Large Digital
	Learning Goals into Scaffolded Lessons 99
	Lessons Learned in the First 20 Days..................102
	Spotlight on Practice: Leading "Meet the Teacher"
	Conferences to Build Trust and Relationships 103
	Families and the First 20 Days........................105
	Spotlight on Practice: Creating Access Points
	for All Students to Thrive Online 106

7	**Leading Live Instruction** 109
	Spotlight on Practice: Developmental Needs
	for Primary Learners.................................110
	Active 112
	Participatory...113
	Spotlight on Practice: Breaking Out of Whole
	Group Meetings into Smaller Discussions............114
	Multimodal...116

Personal 116
Differentiated 117
Spotlight on Practice: Leading Live Instruction
   with Upper Elementary Students 119
Cameras 121

8 Designing Effective Asynchronous Instruction 125
Spotlight on Practice: Designing Accessible and
   Effective Independent Learning Activities 126
Consistent Routines 129
Types of Independent Work 131
Lesson Creation 133
Spotlight on Practice: The Best Tool at Your
   Disposal Is Knowing Your Kids 134
Accessibility 136
Feedback 137
Spotlight on Practice: Using Different Feedback
   Loops for Student Academic and Social-Emotional
   Growth 139

9 Fostering a Home-to-School Connection 143
Learning Coach 144
Spotlight on Practice: A Nana's Journey as a
   Learning Coach and Advocate 145
Onboarding Families 147
Communication 149
    Student-Specific Emails and Messages 149
    Classroom Peek at the Week 149
Spotlight on Practice: Communication Is the
   Key to Working With Families in Online School 150
All School Weekly Newsletter 152
Social Media 152
Volunteering 153
Spotlight on Practice: Family Contributions
   to Community Building 153
Virtual Family Nights 155

10 Creating a Sense of Belonging in Online School 157
   Daily Community Connection 159
      Morning Meeting 159
      Midday Check-in 161
      Closing Circle 162
   Spotlight on Practice: Investing Time in Social
      Emotional Learning and Community 162
   School-Wide Community Building 163
      Spirit Weeks 164
      School Identity 164
      School Rallies 164
      Class Parties 166
      NewsBYTEs News Show 167
      Creating Space for Socialization 167
   Spotlight on Practice: Building Community Through
      Book Clubs 168
   Teacher Moves That Make a Difference 170
   Spotlight on Practice: Scaffolding Play to Build
      Authentic Connections 171

11 Evolving and Growing 175
   Priorities for Building K-5 Online Programs 175
   Spotlight on Practice: Driving Reform in a
      Large System 177
   Next Steps for New Code Academy 179
   Spotlight on Practice: Developing Mutually
      Beneficial Partnerships to Strengthen Your
      Online Program 180
   Next Steps for K-5 Online Learning 182
   Spotlight on Practice: A Music Specialists
      Reflections on Moving Online 183

   Glossary 187
   Appendix 189
   Index 193

Preface

New Code Academy believes every child comes to us with valuable life experiences and perspectives. New Code Academy is committed to a culturally responsive, student-centered environment where learners feel valued, encouraged, and represented in our school community. We provide classroom communities that maximize social skill development and promote academic rigor.

New Code Academy Online School Mission Statement

There is a lack of research and practical resources on K-12 online learning, particularly for the elementary grades of kindergarten through fifth grade. In the spring of 2020, Bloomington Public Schools in Minnesota started to develop a K-12 online school that was launched four months later for the 2020–2021 school year. The effort to create an online school within a traditional school district was a large undertaking and was made possible by staff from across the district, students, and families committed to a similar vision. At the elementary level, the program, most curriculum, professional development, and instruction was all created from scratch. There were frameworks, ideas, and examples that were gleaned from the brick-and-mortar environment, pandemic distance learning resources for secondary grade levels (grades 6–12), and higher education online learning research. However, the components of elementary online education still needed to be put together and tested in action collectively in practice, with kindergarteners nonetheless.

New Code Academy (NCA) elementary, now in its second year, is the successful result of this development. While the school is not perfect—no school is—the program design, pedagogy, and student experience is a point of pride for the school community and has served as a model for other schools and districts who are building online elementary education. The school staff, in partnership with the University of Minnesota's Learning + Technologies Collaborative, has reflected and evaluated on the design, necessary iterations, and nuances of teaching kindergarten through fifth grade students online. Given the lack of resources in this area as well as the questions that are often asked by instructional leaders from other programs, this book serves as a practical contribution to the growing field of K-5 online education.

What's In This Book?

As more teachers and administrators navigate how to offer online learning in elementary settings, this book serves as a resource for pedagogy and program design. The process of building an online program and navigating policies, perceptions, and systems can be isolating and overwhelming for the most experienced and talented instructional leaders. This book overviews the journey—including the pitfalls—of launching NCA and shares tangible instructional ideas and strategies used to teach, engage, and grow elementary students online. The driving question in the creation of this book was: what would have been *helpful and tangible information for instructional leaders and educators to know during the beginnings of building an online school?*

This book encompasses the experience from conception of the idea in spring of 2020, throughout the full first year as a "Bloomington Online School," as well as the rebrand of the school in the summer of 2021 to "New Code Academy," and halfway into the 2021–2022 school year. The chapter topics include categories of the school design elements: introduction to the context and priorities (chapters 1 & 2); the development and design process of the school (chapters 3 & 4); preparing educators and students for online education (chapters 5 & 6); what online instruction looks like at NCA elementary (chapters 7 & 8); a focus on school and home community (chapters 9 & 10); and insights for the future (chapter 11). All of these topics are interconnected, and readers are encouraged to look back and peek forward to find answers to potential questions. Each chapter will share resources (including articles, books, websites) used in the process, details about the NCA elementary schooling model, and spotlights written by the NCA teachers, instructional leaders, and community members. Throughout each chapter there are references to cornerstone research and instructional frameworks that were used to inform decision making and design.

Where Did This Information Come From?

The content of this book highlights and features the ideas, problem solving, and evolution of the Bloomington Public Schools staff and NCA community. This school and what was built is truly a sum of talented and passionate educators who were willing to create something different. This book was curated and composed by Holly Skadsem, the Digital Learning Coordinator and instructional leader of NCA elementary and Lana Peterson, a Research-Practice Partner for NCA from the Learning + Technologies Collaborative at the University of Minnesota. Some information shared in this book was collected during research and evaluation activities, but most is a showcase and retelling from instructional leaders, educators, and family members who experienced it.

Acknowledgements

There is a long list of outstanding educators and human beings that make up the backbone of New Code Academy. Some have contributed their voice within the book's spotlights but there are many more who have made NCA what it is today. Before diving into the details of the school it is important to first and foremost acknowledge all the people who made the school worth writing a book about.

The Digital Learning Team

John Weisser and Katrina Mezera have served as strategic district leaders who have solved complex problems so that instructional leaders and educators could focus on the important work with students. Their leadership paved the way for NCA to exist today and supported the creation of this book. Andrew Rummel served as the NCA secondary instructional lead providing support, encouragement, and problem solving for NCA elementary. Rebecca Brower, NCA K-12 Assistant principal has been influential in the development, day-to-day operations, and culture of our school. Annie Schroeder has envisioned the K-8 computer science component of NCA and works closely with our computer science teachers to guide implementation.

NCA Staff

Our NCA teachers and staff jumped into the unknown feet first with a commitment to excellence. Their talents, fearlessness, sweat, tears, and love for students created a school and experience that some thought was impossible. A heartfelt thank you to this list of courageous, innovative, and dedicated educators: Allison Kalkman, Rachel Mersch, Kristen Fett, Anna Weber, Danika Tranby, Gina Schroeder, Kathy Schneider, Allyson Martinez, Rachel Loy, Sara Loftus, Lisa Cogswell, Melissa Abrahams, Emilee Vlasin, Lorna Duenas, Emily Wahlquist, Tori Nienaltowski, Tara Oldfield, Kristin Bellinger, Kristi Wobbema, Colleen Gunkel, Matt Marohn, Ken Putt, Serena Kamperschroer, Kelly Yurecko, Janelle Berry-Blasingame, Robin Krueger, Raymond Cannon, Whitney Determan, Sara Benson, Tara Sweeney, Nan Lu, Jan Byer, Don Cannon, Angie Fleming, Kari Brue, Joyce Mudgett, Emily Lambrecht, LaTreena Felegy, Annie Caparosa, Caitlin Moodie, Justin Lund, Kelly Anderson, Tammy Kellen, Lisa Harford, Lauri Muñoz, Julie Cohen, Karen Ciesielczyk, Chris Hassenback, Hannah Lott-Havey, Esther Striker, Stephanie Bruggman, Briana Weigel, Kathleen Gustafson, Jennifer Corcoran, Rachael Banz, Carrie Lindgren, Jodi Bresnahan, and Renee Haeuser.

We thank our amazing support staff that have done everything from last-minute Target and UPS runs, to delivering material to families' doors, to making copies and a whole lot more: we are so grateful for you. Thank you Sara Eidam, Carla Richter, and Kim Chroup.

Washburn Elementary Partner School

Thank you to the partner school, Washburn Elementary, for welcoming NCA into your school community and sharing your talented staff. Thank you Andrew Wilkins for fearlessly taking on the role of Principal at both Washburn Elementary and NCA. Thank you Susan Smith, our warm and caring secretary, for taking online students, families, and teachers under your wing. We thank our Equity Specialist, Vianny Rodriguez for serving all families in so many capacities. We have also relied on the support of building staff members Brian Gorman, Daniel Bonin,

Brannon Moore, Elease Darby, Lori Matlon, and Libby Kieser. Thank you.

District Leads

Thank you to the team of talented district professionals who worked tirelessly during the summer of 2020 and throughout the school year to lead and facilitate the development of the online elementary school. Thank you for your incredible leadership: Kerry Young, Laura Ramsborg, Devin Tomczik, Ruth Murray, and Tim Kaari.

Summer Development Team

Thank you to the summer development team that spent hours of time building the interdisciplinary curriculum during the summer of 2020. Thank you for your dedication, curiosity, and commitment to a challenging task. The following staff made it possible for us to start the year: Tricia Adkins, Danielle Andvik, Frederick Ballew, Katie Becker, Adele Binning, Cristin Caruso, Beth Daly, Chris Donley, Jamie Dreyling, Taylor Durry, Kari Govig, Rachel Hansen, Melanie Hendrickson, Jeff Hopkins, Tania Hultengren, Monica Kobold, Alexandra Loosbrock, Stephanie MacPhail, Sarah Maistrovich, Beth McCoy, Matt McDonell, Sharon Mrozek, Taylor Mundis, Lee Nelson, Maddie Nelson, Abby Olson, Gretchen Orth, Linnea Pignatello, Jenny Raabe, Ana Redemann, Anne Roush, Kari Sickman, Jennifer Steffes, Jenna Strandine, Nicole Sundt, Alyssa Vorhees, Johanna Walters, Leanne Wasleske, Ryan Watt, and Emily Wendt.

Our summer development consultants from Bloomington's Office of Educational Equity dedicated summer time to ensuring our curriculum framework was inclusive for all students. Thank you, Chinda Gregor, Abdirahman Hassan, and Niambi Jackson.

University of Minnesota Research Practice Partners

A huge thanks to our Research-Practice Partners from the Learning + Technologies Collaborative at the University of Minnesota Dr. Cassie Scharber, Rukmini Avadhanam, and Farah Faruqi. These talented researchers served as a guiding light during development, collecting data, giving expert insights, and helping the school solve problems of practice. A special thank you to Dr. Scharber for supporting the creation of this book.

Technology Department

Thank you to the Bloomington Public Schools technology and data teams who have supported NCA all along the way. Thank you to Mark Hinton, Sam Raths, our dedicated tech paraprofessional, Kaija Kostamo Tapajna, and the entire tech team for making online school possible by providing a solid infrastructure and device plan for our students. Thank you to the data team—Emmy Moody, Alyssa Holliday, Kathy Pyne, Jake Heiberger, and Danny Leung—who built new data structures and reporting, processed open enrollments in a hurry, and continue to gather important data for our school.

New Code Academy Family Community

Thank you to the parents, guardians, and families that put their trust in the NCA team to take care of their students in a challenging time with many unknowns. A special thank you to the parents that served on the family advisory and dedicated extra time and energy to making the school great: Megan Reams, Eric Stanton, Lindsay Larson, Melissa Klement, Tom Szewczyk, Cathe Lewis, Jessica Moe, Stacy Roberts, Jessica McDonald, Adam McDonald, Veronica Dammeyer, Jessica Dahlton, and Liz Rolfsmeier.

Thank you to the countless volunteers that made it possible to deliver monthly materials, school supplies, and food to the online families including Jefferson High School National Honor Society students led by Erin Lauer, specifically Megan Zheng, Valerie Miller, and Weslee Terry. Thank you to Emily Gagnon who led the Volunteer Connection program and Sandra Mortenson for delivering supplies to families.

Colleagues and Book Reviewers

Thank you to our colleagues who reviewed and provided feedback on the draft of this book. Your thoughtful suggestions, revisions, and insights have made this book stronger. Thank you Troy Anderson, Frederick Ballew, Sarah Barksdale, Ryan Barnick, Katie Baskin, Sean Beaverson, Dave Blanchard, Daryl Boeckers, Dan Bordwell, Tami Brass, Jocelynn Buckentin, Nicole Butler, Kristy Cook, Beth Cramer, Janelle Field, Tracey Hamel, Tina Henely, Nils Hoeger-Lerdal, Glen Irvin, Nicole Joswiak, Angie Kalthoff, David Lostetter, Mary Mehsikomer, Katrina Mezera, Kelsey Nash, Mark Nechanicky, Rachel Pierson, Jeff Plaman, Karen Qualey, Dr. Meagan Rathbun, Andrew Rummel, Audrey Thornborrow, Amy Thuesen, and David Zukor.

Routledge, Taylor Francis Group

Thank you to Daniel Schwartz, our supportive editor for guiding us through the process of our first book. Big thanks and appreciation to all the editors, designers, reviewers, and staff who had a role in making this book.

Our Families

A very big thank you to our families, particularly Adrian, Erik, Annabelle, Clara, Bradley, Lana, Buddy, Deb, Pete and friends who supported us in writing this book while working full time. Your understanding, generosity of time, and encouragement made this project possible.

1

Introduction

This chapter will introduce the local and societal conditions as well as introduce the research-based framework that shaped the design of New Code Academy.

The context of what was happening in the world and the state of the K-12 online learning field during the conception of New Code Academy (NCA) is important as it shaped the school design and process. In the spring of 2020, the COVID-19 pandemic gave most students, teachers, and families around the world an experience in **emergency remote teaching** (Hodges et al., 2020). Bloomington Public Schools also experienced the challenges of delivering equitable instruction from a distance which served as motivation to create an online educational option that provided opportunities for all students to achieve. It was a moment of collective trauma and action. This taste of the online modality as well as the ongoing pandemic (as of the writing of this book), has resulted in a large growth of the field of K-12 online learning, particularly within public school districts who did not have fully online programs prior to the pandemic (Schwartz et al., 2020).

It is important to begin with a distinction between K-12 online learning and emergency remote teaching (ERT) (Hodges et al., 2020). In ERT school districts, teachers, students, and families did what they could with what they had to provide a safe learning environment in response to a pandemic. In the world-wide crash course in delivering instruction from a distance, schools leaned on resources and experience originally designed for technology integration into **brick-and-mortar** classroom learning—if they had it. In contrast, the field of K-12 online learning has been steadily growing since the 1990s, and this learning modality has historically been led by for-profit charter schools (Molnar et al., 2019, 2021). Prior to the pandemic, K-12 fully online learning had been considered a fringe schooling option among predominately wealthier white students who had the means to choose this learning model (Mann, 2019). Some districts offered online schooling, primarily to high schoolers, to fill programming gaps, as a solution to staffing issues, geographic isolation, alternative school option, and credit recovery (Mann et al., 2021; Molnar et al., 2019).

The ERT experience in the spring 2020 and the unknown of the pandemic's trajectory resulted in more families choosing fully online programs. This created an opportunity for students and families to experience a learning model they may have never considered prior to the pandemic and, for some, proved to be the educational environment they wanted long term. Schools and districts around the world are now grappling with how to offer quality online learning programs for the families they serve. One motivating factor in offering these programs includes seeing students who previously struggled academically or behaviorally in physical schooling spaces succeed online. Additionally, districts are analyzing the financial reality of the loss of cost-per-pupil dollars of students leaving the district for online education programs and the impact that could have on already stressed budgets. The resources and research on K-12 online learning is limited, leaving teachers and instructional leaders without guidance about online program design, instructional strategies, curriculum, and staffing within a traditional education system.

Voices from New Code Academy

Throughout each chapter of this book multiple instructional leaders, teachers, and family members will share their voice and experience on the chapter topic through a "Spotlight on Practice." As the creation of NCA elementary is truly a result of significant efforts and contributions from district staff and families, these spotlights showcase the unique perspectives and experiences from many who were involved.

Spotlight on Practice: Should We Build a K-12 Online School by Fall?

Katrina Mezera, Director of Digital Learning and Data, Bloomington Public Schools

In April 2020, our district digital learning team met online to discuss whether or not we should build a K-12 online school by the fall. I remember my thoughts racing as we considered all the implications during the meeting:

Emergency distance learning as a reactionary model to the pandemic had proven to be a difficult switch for our students and staff, but our team knew there was a need and demand for K-12 online learning. It was already in our five-year plan to expand the online learning program at the high-school to the middle-school level. It seemed straightforward to fast track that deliverable, but elementary online school still seemed hard to imagine. Our district is the right size, in that we are big enough to launch a new program like this without causing too much disruption to the overall system. Our digital learning team is often on the leading edge of educational technology movements, and we have built a strong infrastructure for educational technology.

This infrastructure paired with our team's experience, creativity, and teamwork made us all feel more confident in the idea of building a K-12 online school in four months. We briefly considered whether we should buy a program from a vendor, but our philosophy has always been that we believe our teachers can teach and design content better than what can be bought. What we were designing exactly, given the unknowns of timeline and interest, led to more questions than answers. By the end of our meeting the question of **should we** build an online school changed to ***are we*** going to build an online school? To answer this new question we voted, and I was the only one who said no with the qualifier that if I was outvoted by the other three I would be all in.

The next few months flew by in a blur of seemingly infinite questions and decision making:

- **Staffing:** Who would staff the school? How will we select them? Was it a permanent move? What was the criteria?
- **Special Education:** How would students with IEPs be served?
- **Resources:** What curricular materials will we need to keep things hands on? How will they get to students?
- **Professional Development:** How will teachers be supported on this steep learning curve? What do they need to know and be able to do?
- **Leadership:** Would K-12 get its own principal or would we call upon a principal at each level? Who will make the ultimate decisions?
- **Enrollment:** How can we offer enrollment in an equitable fashion knowing that we might not be able to take everyone? Or, how can we staff such that there is room for everyone?
- **Attendance:** What does it mean to attend online? We'd need to track it for accountability, funding, and to make sure kids weren't falling through the cracks.
- **Behavior:** What were the behavior expectations online, and what if there is an issue?
- **Technology:** How will we get enough technology to make sure all our students are 1:1? How will we distribute it? Will everyone have access to the internet?

The year started in a blur. Everything was a decision that needed to be made. Was it the same as our brick-and-mortar school, or was it different because it was online? Nothing was pre-decided, and there was no precedent to refer to.

In early October of 2020, I observed a skilled kindergarten teacher with a screen full of energetic and engaged kindergarten students learning about the letter V. The class was on task and participating, and the mood was happy. The teacher was providing immediate feedback to students practicing the V sound, even to students who were muted. When they signed off, one student unmuted and said to the teacher, "I love you, Mrs.!" In one short month, this kinder class had developed learning routines and caring relationships that would carry them through the year, and I couldn't have been happier that my team had outvoted me.

The Conception of New Code Academy

A group of educators and district leaders began to consider a better solution to ERT as reality grew that the shutdown of society would last more than two weeks in April of 2020. People were stressed and scared, groceries and other basic needs were being delivered to doorsteps by brave frontline workers in masks and gloves, and many community members had not left their homes in over a month. Teachers with high-risk family members were told to quarantine indefinitely for the safety of their children and loved ones, yet faced the possibility of needing to come back to school before the pandemic was over in order to pay their bills. These very real struggles of the unknown were coupled with everyone in the system trying to get through the school year, and the difficult news cycle on how COVID-19 was ravaging the health system, economy, and the human race. It felt imperative that the school district provide a more sustainable answer for those who could not or did not want to go back to brick-and-mortar school.

For context, Bloomington Public Schools is a first-ring suburb bordering Minneapolis, Minnesota and rests on the traditional, ancestral, and contemporary land of the Dakota. It is the fifth largest city in the state and is in the top-20 largest school districts in Minnesota with about 11,000 students. For brick-and-mortar schools, there are ten elementary, three middle, and two high schools. Bloomington is more diverse than most Minnesota schools racially with students identifying as 20% Hispanic or Latino, 0.6% American Indian or Alaska Native, 6% as Asian, 18% Black or African-American, 0.1% Native Hawaiian or Pacific Islander, 46% white, and 8% as two or more races. Additionally 40% of Bloomington Public Schools students qualify for free or reduced lunch, 13% receive English language services, and 17% of students receive special education services (rc.mn.education.gov).

The district has a resourced digital learning department and provides one Chromebook to every student in the 2nd–12th grade; the district purchased versions of learning management systems and tools and technology integrationists assigned to support every school. This is all financially possible via a community technology referendum. Prior to the pandemic, the district had an alternative online and hybrid program (half online and half in person) at the high-school level and was considering how to extend the program into the middle school. At the time, the digital learning team was experiencing pushback on whether online or hybrid learning would be appropriate for middle school students as teachers and administrators struggled to conceptualize the possibility. The infrastructure, resources, and expertise served as a strong foundation on which to build a K-12 online school.

Educators regularly talk and dream about what education *could* look like, but traditional systems can be inflexible and resource-strapped, stopping idyllic plans from becoming reality. 2020 was a moment in time where all ideas were being considered as mindsets were open due to redesigning education on the fly. Before the school year was over, a cross-district group of change-makers was gathered to share their perspective. During the first meeting, the group was asked one question, "If we could start from scratch and build a brand new school, what would we want it to look like?" The group began to brainstorm with online sticky notes, which were grouped by themes, and the ultimate results of this process were four core tenets featured in the image below. These became the starting points for the work to build the program from the ground up including finding the right staff, designing work required for launch, and deciding what resources were needed to make these tenets a reality.

The decision to create the elementary online school was easy. It was the right thing to do for staff, students, and families, but the feelings of doubt began to creep in quickly for the digital learning team. Can elementary students really learn online? Is there any research or frameworks that currently exist that can be learned from? How do we bring these big ideas to life in a virtual space? The district had been partnering with the Learning + Technologies Collaborative (LTC) from the University of Minnesota to build a computer science education pathway and asked the collaborative to expand their research-practice partnership to the development, implementation, and evaluation of the K-12 NCA.

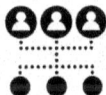
Responsive to student needs, strengths, interests, and aspirations

Interdisciplinary, standards-based approach to unit design

Intentional balance of on-and-off-screen learning activities

Virtual face-to-face experiences to build relationships and community

FIGURE 1.1 Four tenets of NCA elementary, 2020

> **Spotlight on Practice:
> Taking a Leap of Faith to
> Online Teaching**

Rachel Mersch, New Code Academy, Kindergarten Teacher

In early July 2020, we learned that I was pregnant with our third child. Those early days were spent celebrating the exciting news, but my mind quickly wandered toward the matter of health and safety. At the time, the COVID-19 pandemic was still new, and amidst many unknowns, I felt vulnerable. It was not known what model schools would choose, how many transitions we would have, or if I would be protected from contracting COVID-19 and possibly endangering my baby . . . especially as a kindergarten teacher.

As these questions swirled, I wondered if I would be offered accommodations or could work remotely. I quickly realized options for either were slim after reaching out to HR and my doctor. I vaguely remembered hearing news that Bloomington would be trying to create a year-long online school. I previously had no interest in applying to teach remotely for the year, but the news that I was pregnant changed it all. I noticed the application deadline was the same date of my first ultrasound. It felt like the universe was speaking to me: if this pregnancy was a go, it was a sign to go all-in and apply for an online position.

Seeing our baby's tiny heartbeat flickering on the screen motivated me to pour my heart and soul into the application and interview process to try to secure a remote position for fall. After my interview I was filled with nerves and excitement. When Holly called and offered me one of the six online teaching positions, I was both shocked and thrilled. The questions and worries about having to go back to the brick-and-mortar classroom shifted to how I would teach kindergarteners online.

As I sit here and reflect on the school year holding my new baby boy, I could not be more proud of the curriculum we created, the relationships we forged, and the magic we made teaching online. We pioneered a new type of learning for our students and grew our skills as professionals. I first applied to be an online teacher for the safety of my family and continued as an online teacher because I enjoy it, and we designed an educational program that works.

A Day We Will Never Forget

On May 25th, 2020 George Floyd was murdered less than 10 miles from Bloomington. The tragedy and injustice of this event shook the world. Black and brown people have long experienced racial injustice and disproportionate rates of death while in the custody of police, but the events of Mr. Floyd's murder inspired global action and protest. In the weeks after his death, the Twin Cities was the epicenter of marches, dialogues, arrests, arson and looting, community clean up, city-wide curfews, and military occupation. Due to the pandemic, the world was connecting and sharing technologically like never before. Social media feeds and newscasts were filled with calls for people—particularly white people—to learn about, serve as true allies, and take action against racial injustice. This call to action was seen amongst NCA teaching staff who are predominately white women and were more eager than ever before to learn about ways in which they contribute to white supremacy and how they could better serve the needs of Black, Indigenous, Hispanic, and Asian students personally and academically. George Floyd's life mattered, and he should still be alive today.

Guiding Instructional Research and Framework

In parallel with the call to action to address racial injustice, website articles, webinars, podcasts, and technological advances were being published to help schools deliver ERT. While the surge of new resources did provide some ideas for teaching elementary students online, most were focused on the short term pandemic response. There is 20+ years of published research on K-12 online education; yet, most lack rigorous methods and reliable evidence to guide online instructional practices (Molnar, 2021; Prettyman & Sass, 2020). Of what is available, many articles are outdated, focus on a specific tool, or make claims about K-12 online learning when the research studies secondary (6th–12th grade) settings. Additionally, K-12 online learning has been dominated by for-profit charter schools which has led to less access to data and oversight to understand teaching elementary learners online (Molnar, 2021). To build a research-based instructional framework, the NCA elementary instructional leaders and LTC partners looked for connections and intersections between online learning literature, often from the higher education level, and pedagogical approaches from brick-and-mortar elementary schools.

Community of Inquiry

A guiding resource was the Community of Inquiry (COI) model which originated out of higher education (Garrison et al., 1999). This process-oriented model acknowledges that learning is social as well as emotional and that instructional components are interconnected (Cleveland-Innes & Campbell, 2012). The use of the COI model within school planning, teacher professional development, and program evaluation promotes intentionality and reflection about how online learning is being designed. For instance, in the overlap of social and cognitive presence, a guiding question could be the following: how are students given a variety of opportunities to interact together related to class content? Is it just through online meetings, or is there a way to utilize a tool to get students interacting academically? Notably, the educational context—as depicted by the outer circle in the model below—impacts and shapes the community of inquiry.

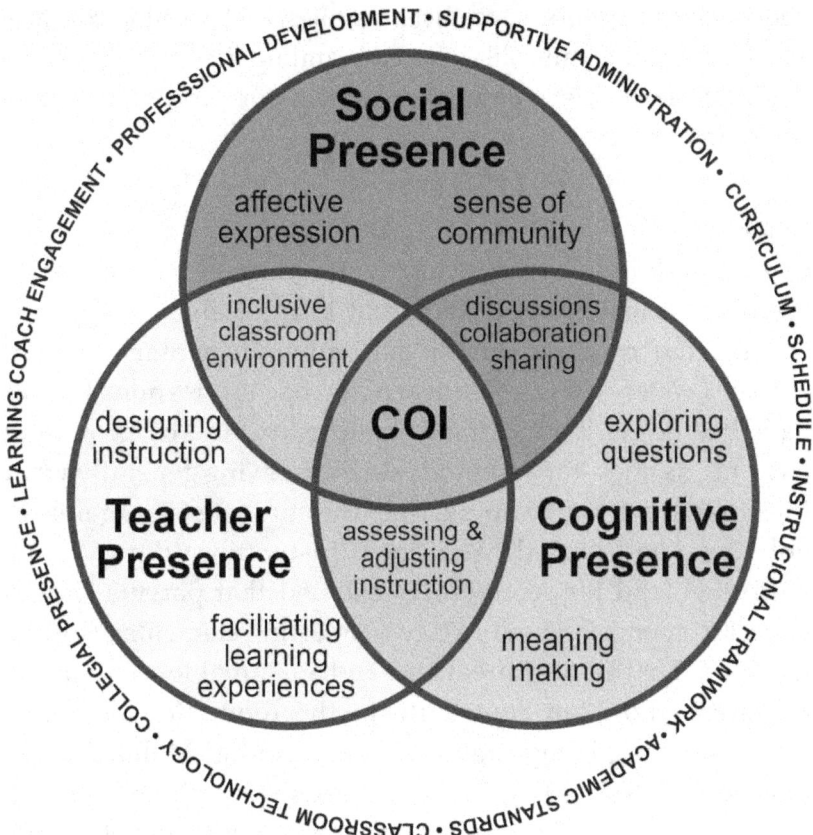

FIGURE 1.2 Community of inquiry model
Source: Adapted from Garrison et al. (1999) and Cleveland-Innes and Campbell (2012)

Sanders and Lokey-Vega (2020) examined the COI model within a high school online social studies course and identified specific instructional practices for each section of the model including: curating supplemental resources, using real-world examples, and building relationships with students. A major finding of this article was how collegial presence was not visible in the higher education COI model. Collegial presence refers to the sense making and processing that happens in K-12 online learning with paraprofessionals, grade-level teacher peers, administrators, specialists, families, and learning coaches. Thus, program features like shared planning time and collaborative professional development are crucial for elementary online programs.

Learning Coach

One key addition to the school community is each student's **learning coach(es)**, often a parent but not always, who are the adult(s) physically with the online elementary student all day (Waters, 2012). The learning coaches' responsibilities have been described as the following: nurture by providing basic needs, monitor and motivate by knowing generally what the student should be doing, help the student stay organized, volunteer, and provide additional instruction (Borup et al., 2014). Lee and Figueroa (2012) claimed that parents should expect to spend 3–5 hours a day supporting elementary online learners. That is an unrealistic and inequitable expectation of parents that can contribute to the reputation of online online learning being digital homeschooling (Molnar, 2019). The field of K-5 online learning needs research on: elementary learning coaches and parent involvement and behaviors; building educator and learning coach partnerships; and how to develop students' independent digital learning skills such as executive functioning and self-regulation so they are less dependent on learning coaches for support.

Cognition and the Brain

Studies about online learning instruction often lead to research on cognition, particularly the Cognitive Load Theory, which refers to the constant reorganization the brain is doing as new concepts enter and are added to memory (Sands, 2019; Sweller, 1988). This focus on neuroscience in online learning draws interest due to the sheer amount of information, visuals, and potential distractions that students may experience via the computer. Educators are unable to control the physical environment in online learning such as reducing noise and directing attention—particularly when students are working independently—so there is a stronger focus on brain and cognition science when designing lessons and activities.

Built on the three stages of brain processing—input, elaboration, and application as well as culturally responsive information processing techniques—Zaretta Hammond's "ignite, chunk, chew, and review" became a core instructional approach for NCA elementary (2015, pp. 129–138). The first strategy <u>ignite</u> tells the brain it is time to learn and Hammond recommends storytelling, chants, music, provocations, and discussions to get the brain's attention. Next, students experience a <u>chunk</u> of new information via the teacher, a reading, or a peer that is small enough to process. "Chunking" content into small segments, removing unnecessary information, highlighting key information, and multimodal media are common strategies in online learning (Brame, 2015).

The third strategy, <u>chew</u>, is a two-step approach by first giving students unstructured think time to process the new information. Pre-teaching cognitive routines or thinking maps can equip students with deeper processing tools. The second part of the <u>chew</u> strategy is the active processing with peers, through performance, verbal activities, developing visuals, and word play. Hammond's fourth strategy is for students to review new knowledge through application and practice within 24 hours of learning. Reviewing new content through games, problem solving, and working on authentic projects strengthens their neural pathways and promotes dendrite growth. This cognitive approach combined with culturally responsive input, elaboration, and application strategies builds intellectual capacity for students.

> **Spotlight on Practice:**
> **Key Aspects of High-Quality**
> **Learning Experiences**

Jeff Plaman, Online and Digital Learning Specialist – Minnesota Department of Education

As the Online and Digital Learning Specialist at the Minnesota Department of Education, I have the privilege of working with our public online schools who, since the mid-90s, have provided enrollment options for families across Minnesota. Prior to March of 2020, the number of elementary-aged students enrolled in our online schools has remained relatively stable at around 1600 students.

When the COVID-19 pandemic required the closure of school buildings, every student got to experience emergency distance learning, for better or worse. Recent data indicates, however, that even as the health concerns of the pandemic recede, many students, and in particular students of color, will participate in online education opportunities (Saavedra et al., 2021).

There has been no shortage of Minnesota public schools responding to the needs of their students. In March 2020, Minnesota had 38 state-approved online public schools. Typically two or three new applications per year are processed by our office. As of December 2021, there were 385 schools and districts who had been provisionally approved to provide online education in the 21–22 school year. Of those, 35 are pursuing applications to join the existing 63 state-approved online providers.

Providing an excellent online education for elementary students does not follow a one-size-fits-all formula. In fact, that is both a strength and potential pitfall for professionals developing online programs. *How do you personalize instruction while at the same time ensure that students are meeting required academic standards and benchmarks and social-emotional learning targets?*

As more schools and districts design online programs and seek advice for instructional design, I always share these three key aspects of high-quality online experiences:

Relationships: The Internet connects devices, and the people who operate them together; it is fundamentally built to enable seamless connection. As much as possible, online education should encourage interactions and relationship development between students, teachers, and families. Students should be engaging with other students, their teachers and caregivers multiple times per day not just in task-oriented ways, thereby creating opportunities for playful interaction.

Structure and Flexibility: Online learning can provide flexibility where students have some element of control over time, place, path, and pace. At the same time, we know that learners need structure in varying degrees based on their age, maturity level, experience, subject matter, interest, and a host of other factors that may affect their engagement. Knowing each learner (see Relationships) is essential to design experiences that work for them, but there are some design choices that should be considered:

1. Clear and consistent design, not cluttered
2. Blend synchronous and asynchronous modalities
3. Active communication

Assessment for and of Learning: Knowing a student's current level of understanding (assessment), skill, or knowledge requires intentional design online because you don't usually have the ability to see a puzzled look on someone's face indicating they don't understand or seeing them doodling which may be an indicator that they're bored and not challenged at the right level. Every "nugget" of learning that you design has to include some form of assessment both for the students to check their own level of understanding but also as information to the teacher that informs the next moves that they make.

Culturally Responsive Teaching

Culturally responsive teaching is a brain- and asset-based approach to creating an effective learning environment with high standards for learners. There have been evolutions of culturally responsive teaching in research and practice but contemporary experts describe the pedagogy as culturally proficient educators who understand and address how culture impacts what happens in learning spaces, understand how the brain works and use effective instructional strategies, and create an inclusive learning environment (Hammond, 2015; Hollie, 2018; Lindsey et al., 2018).

Universal Design for Learning

Another brain-based approach to designing instruction is Universal Design for Learning (UDL), a framework for accessibility and eliminating inequities by rejecting the "one size fits all" approach that much of education is built upon (Chardin & Novak, 2020). The three core principles of the framework are 1) multiple means of engagement, 2) multiple means of representation, and 3) multiple means of action and expression (CAST, 2018). The neuroscience-driven framework acknowledges the variability amongst learners, encourages variety and flexibility, and discourages lowering expectations (Gronneberg & Johnston, 2015). The full UDL guidelines provide recommendations for recruiting interest, sustaining effort and persistence, self-regulation, perception, language and symbols, comprehension, physical action, expression and communication, and executive functions (CAST, 2018). Combining culturally responsive teaching and UDL encourages educators to move beyond the conversation of access; and instead, connect how offering and honoring multiple means of engagement, representation, and expression could welcome students' identity, funds of knowledge (cultural heritage and home learning), and reduce ableism (Chardin & Novak, 2020).

Elementary Learners

The community and brain-based research was paired with NCA teachers' elementary education experience and effective strategies from the brick-and-mortar classroom. This included developmentally appropriate social and emotional learning, kinesthetic, differentiating and personalizing instruction, gradual release through formative assessment, and interdisciplinary project-based curriculum. The guidance from the research combined with the teachers expertise led to the actualization of NCA's core tenets.

The context of what was happening in the world, coupled with the school's core tenets, research-based instructional framework, and teacher's expertise on elementary learners identifies that; 1) community and relationships are essential; 2) cognition should inform design of lessons and student work; and, there are a multitude of interconnected factors that shape schools. All of these findings are true whether teaching online or in person. The challenge became how to ensure these frameworks were used in program design, professional development, and instruction as NCA launched.

Some Questions to Consider as a Team or Individually When Conceptualizing an Online Elementary School:
- What is your school or district's motivation for starting an online program?
- If you could start from scratch and build a brand new school, what would you want it to look like?
- What instructional frameworks guide your belief about learning and how might they apply in an online learning setting?
- What might be some organizational, political, logistical, or community hurdles that will need to be navigated?

References

Borup, J., West, R. E., Graham, C. R., & Davies, R. S. (2014). The adolescent community of engagement framework: A lens for research on K-12 online learning. *Journal of Technology and Teacher Education, 22*(1), 107–129.

Brame, C. J. (2015). *Effective educational videos*. Vanderbilt University. http://cft.vanderbilt.edu/guides-sub-pages/effective-educational-videos/

CAST. (2018). *Universal design for learning guidelines version 2.2*. http://udlguidelines.cast.org

Chardin, M., & Novak, K. (2020). *Equity by design: Delivering on the power and promise of UDL*. Corwin Press.

Cleveland-Innes, M., & Campbell, P. (2012). Emotional presence, learning, and the online learning environment. *The International Review of Research in Open and Distributed Learning, 13*(4), 269–292.

Garrison, D. R., Anderson, T., & Archer, W. (1999). Critical inquiry in a text-based environment: Computer conferencing in higher education. *The Internet and Higher Education, 2*(2–3), 87–105.

Gronneberg, J., & Johnston, S. (2015). 7 things you should know about universal design for learning [Brief]. *Educause Learning Initiative*. https://library.educause.edu/-/media/files/library/2015/4/eli7119-pdf.pdf

Hammond, Z. (2015). *Culturally responsive teaching and the brain: Promoting authentic engagement and rigor among culturally and linguistically diverse students*. Corwin Press.

Hodges, C., Moore, S., Lockee, B., Trust, T., & Bond, A. (2020). The difference between emergency remote teaching and online learning. *Educause Review, 27*(1), 1–9.

Hollie, S. (2018). *Culturally and linguistically responsive teaching and learning: Classroom practices for student success*. Shell Education.

Lee, M., & Figueroa, R. (2012). Internal and external indicators of virtual learning success: A guide to success in K-12 virtual learning. *Distance Learning, 9*(1), 21.

Lindsey, R. B., Nuri-Robins, K., Terrell, R. D., & Lindsey, D. B. (2018). *Cultural proficiency: A manual for school leaders*. Corwin Press.

Mann, B. (2019). Whiteness and economic advantage in digital schooling: Diversity patterns and equity considerations for K-12 online charter schools. *Education Policy Analysis Archives, 27*(105). https://doi.org/10.14507/epaa.27.4532

Mann, B., Li, W., & Besnoy, K. (2021). Digital divides: K-12 student profiles and online learning. *Education Policy Analysis Archives, 29*(112). https://doi.org/10.14507/epaa.29.6351

Molnar, A., Miron, G., Barbour, M. K., Huerta, L., Shafer, S. R., Rice, J. K., Glover, A., Browning, N., Hagle, S., & Boninger, F. (2021). *Virtual schools in the U.S. 2021*. National Education Policy Center.

Molnar, A., Miron, G., Elgeberi, N., Barbour, M. K., Huerta, L., Shafer, S. R., & Rice, J. K. (2019). *Virtual schools in the US 2019*. National Education Policy Center.

Prettyman, A., & Sass, T. R. (2020). *The efficacy of virtual instruction in K-12 education: A review of the literature*. Georgia Policy Labs, Metro Atlanta Policy Lab for Education.

Saavedra, A., Rapaport, A., & Silver, D. (2021). *Why some parents are sticking with remote learning—even as schools reopen*. Brown Center Chalkboard. https://www.brookings.edu/blog/brown-center-chalkboard/2021/06/08/why-some-parents-are-sticking-with-remote-learning-even-as-schools-reopen

Sanders, K., & Lokey-Vega, A. (2020). K-12 community of inquiry: A case study of the applicability of the community of inquiry framework in the K-12 learning environment. *Journal of Online Learning Research, 6*(1), 35–56.

Sands, P. (2019). Addressing cognitive load in the computer science classroom. *ACM Inroads, 10*(1), 44–51.

Schwartz, H. L., Grant, D., Diliberti, M. K., Hunter, G. P., & Setodji, C. M. (2020). *Remote learning is here to stay: Results from the first American school district panel survey*. Research Report. RR-A956-1. RAND Corporation.

Sweller, J. (1988). Cognitive load during problem solving: Effects on learning. *Cognitive Science, 12*(2), 257–285.

Waters, L. H. (2012). *Exploring the experiences of learning coaches in a cyber charter school: A qualitative case study* [Doctoral dissertation, University of Hawaii] (1347666490). ProQuest Dissertation Publishing.

2

Establishing a Lens of Equity and Social Justice

As schools and districts build their online learning programs, equity needs to be the first priority within the design process. The following chapter will introduce an equity framework and considerations for access, achievement, identity, and power within online schooling.

Prior to the pandemic, K-12 online schools—which were primarily for-profit charter schools—had a higher percentage of white and socioeconmically advantaged students compared to brick-and-mortar public schools. Moreover, these online schools have consistently not performed as well on standardized tests compared to brick-and-mortar schools (Mann, 2019; Prettyman & Sass, 2020). The industry grew around its customer base and continues to lack oversight in how to equitably serve all students based on their race, culture, socio-economic status, disability, and geographic location (Mann, 2019). While emergency remote teaching (ERT) (Hodges et al., 2020) that took place in response to the pandemic is not the same as online learning, it illuminated long-standing disparities around the type of student who could access and succeed in current approaches to distance learning (Oster et al., 2021). Related, and critical to our context at NCA, Minnesota has one of the worst achievement gaps in the country between races, ethnicities, and socio-economic status in achievement and graduation rates (Grunewald & Nath, 2019). To build something radically different, prioritizing equity and the perspectives of historically marginalized students needed to be the foundation of New Code Academy's approach.

What is Equity?

This word equity has become somewhat of a buzzword that gets included in plans and communication without clarity. Rochelle Gutiérrez is an influential math education scholar whose framing of equity guided the development and evaluation of NCA. She defines equity using four necessary dimensions: access, achievement, identity, and power (2012).

Access

Access and achievement are Guiterrez's *dominant* dimensions of equity that allow students to "play the game" of school that society has created (Gutiérrez, 2012, p. 20). The issues in these dominant dimensions often feel more solvable and are more comfortable for educators and school leaders to consider; NCA instructional leaders are likely guilty of over-focusing on these dimensions as well. Given the historical disparities in access to online schooling, NCA invested a significant amount of energy and thought into ensuring students and families had physical resources. Students are provided tablets, reliable wifi, monthly learning materials (see Chapter 4), and any additional resources on a need-by-need basis to have equal access to online learning. For example, NCA's social worker has secured families from around the state of MN resources such as microphones to block out background noise, warm winter clothing, and food sources in their home communities. If students regularly receive basic needs from school, it could be a deterrent to attend online if that would impact student access to the services they need to survive.

The goal was for NCA to be racially and culturally representative of the district's student population to ensure all learners who wanted to participate online had access. NCA provided the district Office of Educational Equity (OEE) information about the program so that specialists could respond to questions families might have. To ensure NCA's families had access to information in their home languages to support their child, a process and routine was created to translate all weekly communication. NCA's learning management system, Seesaw and communication app, Remind, both have language translation features for families that need it. While these efforts are a start, improving access is an ongoing process, and there are still problems to solve in this area, particularly since in year two NCA students are now geographically dispersed across the state. The work to provide access means nothing if students are not able to find success within the program.

Spotlight on Practice: Knowing Learners Culturally, Academically, and Personally to Build Equitable Instruction

Colleen Gunkel, New Code Academy, Fifth Grade Teacher

To address inequities within online learning you must first know your students culturally, academically, and personally. In addition to building relationships through our meet the teacher conferences, I asked families to fill out a culture survey and then chose four topics from the survey that we asked students to share about during the year. I created the survey in my Master's program and used prompts from Sharocky Hollie's "Culturally and Linguistically Responsive Teaching and Learning: Classroom Practices for Student Success" and the process from Responsive Classroom's "Dialogue Sharing" approach. When it was a student's day to share about the topic, they might bring possessions that have personal meaning. Once each student brought a family or community member in for one of the topics. This activity showed my kids I value their culture, it built a trust and community amongst our class, and helped me personalize the learning environment all year.

1. Why do you have the name that you have? What is the meaning of your name?
2. What place best describes your culture or family?
3. What object in your home best describes your culture or family?
4. What is your favorite tradition in your family?
5. Name a family member or community member who you admire. Explain why.

My fifth grade teaching partner and I were intentional about using our whole group meets for community building and taught all new lessons asynchronously. This allowed us to carve out 45 minutes for small group, differentiated math each day. Together we team-taught throughout the year to provide more individualized instruction that met students' needs through flexible math and reading small groups. Within these small groups, we were able to use the information shared from the culture survey to connect and differentiate with our learners.

For example, in math we would have every student do a pre-assessment on a specific standard using Google Forms. We grouped students based on their needs related to that standard and designed interventions and activities that we thought would be most valuable. Having more students from two classes to create groups served as a benefit as there were more overlaps in need. We designed our math curriculum to be self-paced and used the Google Forms and the data dashboards on IXL and Khan Academy to select and design math interventions and enrichment based on student need. Additionally, we would do one-on-one mastery checks with students for each standard which provided further insight into their needs as learners.

Working as a team with my grade level colleague reduced the amount of work for us as educators since we could combine our capacity to meet the range of academic needs. Having two educators consider all of the students by using groups based on performance with each standard (rather than arbitrary leveled groups) and knowing our students as people and learners created more equitable instruction. This team approach and the reduced distractions during small group instruction online resulted in my students receiving more individualized and differentiated instruction than they did in the brick-and-mortar classroom.

Achievement

To support all students in being online learners, the first 20 days are focused on ensuring that students have relationships, digital competencies, and understanding of routines (see Chapter 6). This time affords teachers an opportunity to learn what motivates and engages students, and to adapt instruction to push them to grow academically. The schedule includes a lot of small group and differentiated instruction informed by formative assessments, and many teachers have shared the intimacy of online meeting rooms has led to more and richer instructional time. Within the **independent learning assignments**, teachers use multimodal instructions through video, audio, symbols, and text to remove any barriers that reading or language can create. The design of the online learning should not prevent students from achieving academically but rather strive to accelerate learning (see Chapter 8). Availability of adult support during independent work time can create inequities, and NCA has developed a connected model where students don't need to sign out and can receive additional academic support from specialist teachers (music, physical education, and art) when completing independent work.

While standardized testing is just one star in the galaxy for understanding student achievement, there is interest amongst instructional leaders and researchers in understanding how NCA students are achieving academically in comparison to their brick-and-mortar peers. Due to the fluctuations in learning models for schools due to emergency remote teaching and quarantining classes in the 2020–2021 school year, there is not viable data to make any sort of comparison just yet. Anecdotally, some NCA teachers shared that during year one of NCA they saw more growth and students reading on grade level than they had previously in the brick-and-mortar classroom.

Identity

Beyond the dominant dimensions of access and achievement, Gutiérrez (2012) encourages educators and researchers to consider the *critical* dimensions of identity and power. Rather than teach kids how to "play the game of school" by fitting into one model of school; how can schools *with* students "change the game" by building instruction around students and embedding opportunities for them to think critically about their world and what is known (p. 21)? To explore this question, staff participate in monthly equity and social justice professional development led by the NCA social justice committee. For example, the 2020 curriculum design team read one of five articles about anti-racist and culturally responsive teaching practices and then used "Five Paradigm Shifts for Equitable Educators" to process (Gorski, 2017). The educators used an interactive online whiteboard to identify quotes that resonated with them, ask questions, be vulnerable, and consider the implications for online schooling. Pairing resources with opportunities to reflect and contemplate the critical equity dimensions is led monthly by the social justice committee.

In addition to educator professional development, OEE consulted with the instructional leaders and educators during the summer curriculum design work (see Chapter 3). Together the group developed a set of questions that would be included on lesson and unit planning templates and staff professional development to pause and consider when designing instruction:

- Whose perspective/voice is represented? Whose perspective/voice is missing?

- How can my students bring their values/strengths into this unit/lesson/activity?
- Is this practice/activity inclusive of different kinds of success?
- Can all students access/understand the directions/activity/information/resource?
- What stereotypes might be introduced or reinforced by the use of this resource/content/activity?
- Where can we build opportunities for students to give feedback?
- Where can we provide opportunities for families to get involved?
- Have we humanized children by recognizing what they have been through this summer?

It was essential for teachers to see and be prompted on these questions often because, as Gutiérrez (2012) shares, equity is contextual. Every student has a unique, intersectional identity with their own life experiences and personality. While there are equitable pedagogical strategies that can work across different classrooms, teachers knowing their students through meaningful relationship building and creating an inclusive and welcoming environment by utilizing the questions like those above is essential. The process of teacher and student partnerships will be new and nuanced every year and requires an educator to be committed to the work it takes. Related, an OEE representative helped to develop questions and served on the interview team tasked with hiring the online elementary teachers. The interview prompt, "identify ways you address stereotypes in your classroom and/or bring anti-bias practices in your classroom," proved to be the deciding factor for multiple candidates as NCA instructional leaders wanted a staff committed to the critical dimensions of equity.

> **Spotlight on Practice: Sometimes the Best Professional Development Includes "Unlearning"**

Emilee Vlasin, New Code Academy, Third Grade Teacher

The social justice committee was created during the launch of NCA to create a culturally responsive, student-centered environment where learners feel valued, encouraged, and represented in our school community. We also focus on helping staff and students on their individual journeys to "unlearn" bias. Our approach rejects blaming, shaming, and guilt and instead focuses on the belief that growth comes from challenging our thinking. The committee led the staff through a reflection on the history and origins of their personal bias by using the "Cycle of Socialization" (Harro, 2000). Staff shared with their peers how racism, ableism, sexism, etc. were introduced and reinforced in their lives as well as the eventual exit through new life experiences from the cycle. By identifying where and how oppressive beliefs entered our lives, we can then begin to "unlearn" these mindsets. From there, each staff member developed their own social justice statement to identify what is important for us personally and professionally. Once the groundwork for social justice was established, we provided monthly choice boards of articles, videos, and resources for staff to continue their unlearning.

One of our main functions as a committee is to ensure that students all have access to "windows and mirrors" in their educational experience (Style, 1996): mirrors being able to see themselves and connect with the topic or context within the classroom curriculum and activities, and windows being the opportunity to learn about other cultures, places, and ideas they have not been introduced to yet. A big part of providing windows and mirrors for students is helping the staff grow to be the educators their students need them to be through knowing better and doing better. Examples of this include ensuring school functions such as class parties and celebrations did not align with holidays and were filled with inclusive activities, as well as providing staff with a template to analyze educational materials for the central message and consider who the characters are.

Another contribution of the social justice committee was providing teachers with guidance and lessons to talk about issues and events that were happening in our world. The night of the insurrection on the U.S. Capitol on January 6th, 2021, had NCA teachers scrambling as they were trying to process the historical event themselves and unsure how to discuss it in class, as they knew it also impacted their students and would likely be brought up. The social justice committee had an emergency meeting and created a response kit of resources for our staff that included:

- Developmentally appropriate check-ins to see how students are feeling
- Discussion tools for navigating important conversations that focused on the various needs of students and encouraged adults to refrain from showing personal beliefs
- Classroom books and videos to help students make sense of things
- Guidance from professionals including district social workers, counselors, and equity liaisons and research published by national organizations focused on student mental health

The social justice committee's everyday duties are to be aware of what is happening in the world and local community and consider how it may impact our students and staff as well as hold ourselves and school policies accountable for what is best for our students. During the 2021–22 school year, online students who qualified for free and reduced lunch were no longer going to be able to access food due to distribution costs. Our leadership and social justice committee fought back against this policy for our students and had the decisions overturned. The goosebumps feeling of ensuring students have what they need to learn reinforces the importance of this committee's work.

Power

Disrupting the status quo of power within schooling happens in big and noticeable as well as nuanced and everyday ways. An intentional choice related to identity and power at NCA was the building of an interdisciplinary, project-based curriculum. The curriculum was designed using themes, big ideas, and essential questions that connect the content to the real world and requires students to think critically about issues in their community. These inquiry-based units create opportunities for students to "be themselves and better themselves" (Gutiérrez, 2012, p. 20) by bringing in their perspective and growing through considering the perspective of others. The four school-wide unit titles include: 1) Systems and Structures, 2) Interactions and Interdependence, 3) Power and Influence, 4) Change and Continuity.

Example Unit Outline

Unit 3: Power and Influence

Big Ideas:
- Looking at our world and our subject areas through the lenses of power and influence
- What role does power and influence play in our world and daily life?
- Learning about multiple perspectives through each subject area

Sample Essential Questions that Students Explore:
- **Kindergarten:** What do I want to learn?
- **Grade 1:** How does asking and answering questions help us learn?
- **Grade 2:** How can people share power, and what power do I have?

- **Grade 3:** How can traits impact self, others and the surrounding environment?
- **Grade 4:** How does knowing and understanding human emotions benefit me?
- **Grade 5:** How might our choices, perspectives, and variables influence how we interact with the world?

Sample End of Unit Projects:
- **Kindergarten:** Develop a cultural suitcase by sharing photos and recordings of their favorite foods, clothing, music, family traditions, and more to reflect on the strengths you bring to the classroom community.
- **Grade 2:** Students complete a research paper on an animal of their choice that connects to their study of Indigenous people of Minnesota.
- **Grade 5:** Use the breaking news feature in WeVideo to record an interview. Work in a group of two to three to create questions for the debate. Interview colonists to learn their different points of view.

Exploring the essential questions within the curriculum without a diverse student population to provide multiple perspectives would limit the experiences of all students. The NCA elementary model prioritizes community building through synchronous meetings, a programmatic design element that is often missing in K-12 online learning (Mann, 2019). Diverse classrooms benefit all students by disrupting systemic power inequities through building relationships with people who look, sound, live, and believe differently than them (Mann, 2019; Orfield & Ee, 2017). For instance, the fifth grade classes noticed the books they were reading were missing characters and authors that were Black, Indigenous, and People of Color. The students used a spreadsheet to document the races of the characters and analyze who had power, whose voice is represented, and who/what was missing or left out of each story. Following a discussion of the findings students found new books with diverse authors and main characters.

In addition to the curriculum, classroom management was an intentional as well as unintentional way power was disrupted in the school. At the beginning of the year, NCA staff discussed traditional behavior management strategies and how this approach conflicts with providing equitable instruction. The school adopted trauma-informed care and conscious discipline as equitable alternatives that focus on the use of language with students. One unintentional disruption of power was the freedom online learning provides to students to control their bodies without impacting other learners. If an online student needs to stand up, sit in a hammock, bring their tablet outside, bounce a ball against the wall, yell out, or make noise, they can do these things without impacting other students' learning. The constant power struggle within brick-and-mortar schools between adults and students about behavior and controlling student bodies reduces greatly in the online environment. This has led to staff conversations about "unlearning" misconceptions about traditional classroom management strategies and frameworks that lack cultural responsiveness and perpetuate the need for control and power in the classroom.

While NCA's instructional leaders and educators have been intentional about creating an equitable online learning environment, it is not perfect and more needs to be done. Beyond getting to know students, teachers and instructional leaders must "critically assess the racial and economic logics and norms driving their practices through conversations" and identify how instruction, technology platforms, and embedded norms reflect the socio-economic and racial customer base online learning has been built for (Mann, 2019, p. 18). Identifying a team, like NCA's social justice committee, and ensuring this team has regular time with staff and also serves on instructional leadership committees can keep the critical assessment at the center of program development and policy decisions.

Questions to Consider Related to Equity in Online Schooling (adapted from Gutiérrez, 2012):

- Who are the students, and what contextual factors shape the way equitable education needs to be built?
- What resources and school structures do students need access to?
- What student outcomes and support will lead to achievement for your students?
- What windows and mirrors will exist within the curriculum?
- How can critical citizenship be built through considering power in everyday life?
- How are the school's norms, instructional practices, and technology platforms perpetuating inequities?

References

Gorski, P. (2017). *Five paradigm shifts for equitable education*. Equity Literacy Institute. https://www.equityliteracy.org/copy-of-approaches-to-equity

Grunewald, R., & Nath, A. (2019, October). *A statewide crisis: Minnesota's education achievement gaps*. Federal Reserve Bank of Minneapolis.

Gutiérrez, R. (2012). Context matters: How should we conceptualize equity in mathematics education? In *Equity in discourse for mathematics education* (pp. 17–33). Springer.

Harro, B. (2000). The cycle of socialization. *Readings for Diversity and Social Justice, 2*, 45–51.

Hodges, C., Moore, S., Lockee, B., Trust, T., & Bond, A. (2020). The difference between emergency remote teaching and online learning. *Educause Review, 27*(1), 1–9.

Mann, B. (2019). Whiteness and economic advantage in digital schooling: Diversity patterns and equity considerations for K-12 online charter schools. *Education Policy Analysis Archives, 27*(105). https://doi.org/10.14507/epaa.27.4532

Orfield, G., & Ee, J. (2017). *Our segregated capital: An increasingly diverse city with racially polarized schools*. Civil Rights Project/Proyecto Derechos Civiles.

Oster, E., Jack, R., Halloran, C., Schoof, J., McLeod, D., Yang, H., Roche, J., & Roche, D. (2021). Disparities in learning mode access among K – 12 students during the COVID-19 pandemic, by race/ethnicity, geography, and grade level – United States, September 2020 – April 2021. *Morbidity and Mortality Weekly Report*, *70*(26), 953.

Prettyman, A., & Sass, T. R. (2020). *The efficacy of virtual instruction in K-12 education: A review of the literature*. Georgia Policy Labs, Metro Atlanta Policy Lab for Education.

Style, E. (1996). Curriculum as window and mirror. *Social Science Record*, *33*(2), 21–28.

3

Building the Foundation of New Learning

This chapter will overview the work that took place during the summer of 2020, three months prior to launching New Code Academy elementary including building the curriculum, hiring and onboarding teachers, and recruiting families. Developing a school (online or brick-and-mortar) in three months is a very short timeline and not recommended beyond emergency situations.

Purchasing vs. Building Curriculum

Schools and districts can purchase curriculum from an established online provider that can be used either through the provider's online platform or integrated into the district's learning management system. The purchased online curriculum is generally through a subscription model that costs hundreds of dollars per "course," or in elementary terms, each subject, and additional money for each student per year. One of the estimates received in the summer of 2020 was $78,000 for 450 students per year. Most of the purchasable curriculum the digital learning team reviewed at the time was set up in modules that students complete independently online. An extension of the purchased curriculum offered by some companies is to contract with them to hire the teachers.

Bloomington Public Schools chose instead to invest curriculum dollars in hiring teams of district teachers to develop curriculum. The purchasable curriculum did not align with the school's core tenets as it was all computer based, prioritized consumption over creation, and lacked the teacher presence within lessons that the team felt was important for elementary learners. Transitioning kindergarten through fifth grade schooling completely online was still difficult for many who were involved in the development to imagine. However, building curriculum internally gave the group more confidence in ensuring academic and social emotional needs would be met. Financially and sustainably, it was a stronger return on investment to have experienced local educators, who know district students, academic standards, and who are committed to culturally responsive pedagogy build a curriculum than pay for a subscription model. The choice to build curriculum might not be best short term or long term for every school due to the size of the program, staffing limitations, and experience with online pedagogies.

School Design Teams

In order to accomplish the multitude of tasks needed to launch the online school in the fall, several teams were formed to work on different projects, the biggest of which was designing the curriculum. The launch and design of the online school was led by the district's Digital Learning Team which included Holly Skadsem, the Elementary Digital Coordinator who led the NCA elementary (grades K-5) development. Holly coordinated the summer design process teams including a cross-department lead team, curriculum design team of district educators, University

TABLE 3.1 NCA Summer 2020 School Design Team Descriptions

School Design Teams	Members	Responsibilities
Digital Learning Team	Instructional arm of technology department and founders of district online school	Met weekly to solve high-level problems, program iterations, communication, budgeting
Lead Team	District specialists from English Language, Special Education, Gifted & Talented, Curriculum and Instruction, and Technology Departments	Met weekly to reflect on progress of grade-level groups and plan meetings. Supported grade-level curriculum development.
Curriculum design team	30 grade-level teachers, specialists from music, art, and physical education, English Language and special education. Grouped in grade-level sub teams	Met weekly project-wide and as needed grade-level meetings. Worked collaboratively and independently on interdisciplinary curriculum design tasks
Office of Educational Equity	Three representatives from the district-wide department	Provide guidance and feedback on curriculum design choices and topics for grade-level groups
University of Minnesota Research-Practice Partners	Researchers and educators from the Learning + Technology Collaborative	Co-solve problems of practice, review literature and resources, co-develop and present professional development

research-practice partners, and consultations with the district's Office of Educational Equity.

The lead team's involvement in the school design provided cross-departmental input in its launch—creating a district-wide sense of ownership of this school. This decision proved essential to success for the program as each lead team member was instrumental in supporting teachers, meeting with families, and helping communication flow throughout the district. The biggest team was the curriculum design team who were recruited through information sessions that communicated the objective and process of the summer work, as well as the message that building the interdisciplinary curriculum did not ensure or require district teachers to be NCA teachers for the fall of 2020. The large team was broken into sub-groups by grade levels and were given concrete roles based on time availability.

> **Spotlight on Practice:**
> **Permission and Compassion**

Kerry Young, NCA Lead Team & English Learner Program Specialist, Bloomington Public Schools

As I reflect on my experience leading and coaching groups of teachers through curriculum building and their transition to becoming online teachers, two themes come to mind: <u>permission</u> and <u>compassion</u>. Our teachers needed the permission and supportive environment to do things differently because online school needed to be different. A lot of our teachers are rule followers, by temperament or because of their own success in traditional schooling environments. Many had never really been given the space and opportunity to try new things within their profession. Our curriculum development team and NCA staff were perfectly poised to be imaginative as we built something that was new to all of us.

Some contextual factors that created <u>permission</u> included that the design of the school was values-driven. Using our core tenets and academic standards as parameters, it gave us the freedom to think creatively rather than changing one element in an already tightly built system. Additionally, there was a benefit in having educators on the curriculum design team that were not going to join the NCA staff online as it allowed them not to get lost in the details of implementation. The development and coaching process was primarily driven from middle-level leaders. Our leadership team lacked the responsibilities and constraints that can weigh down top-level leaders who can get stuck on granular details.

The spring of 2020 gave us all experience in distance learning which primarily was teachers recreating the brick-and-mortar classroom environment online knowing it would be a temporary experience. The NCA curriculum design team and teachers were motivated in building a program that would continue beyond the pandemic. Contextually, societal events including the pandemic and the murder of George Floyd were front and center in all of our lives. A robust, interdisciplinary curriculum that is based on essential questions and enduring understandings provides opportunities for students to think critically and have conversations about the world around them.

As leaders, we have to have <u>compassion</u> for teachers because change and trying new things, especially if the teacher was successful in the traditional environment, can be hard for them. Letting go of effective teacher practices that do not translate online is a process, so showing care and encouraging them to have compassion for themselves and their learners is essential. We have to make space for feeling frustration and overwhelmed because this is different; it's going to feel hard, and it will not be like things they have done before.

There were a lot of NCA teachers who felt successful that first year despite the stress and newness in their job, especially those who did not try to recreate what they were doing in the brick-and-mortar classroom and gave themselves permission to try new things and fail. It was hard and stressful but they were invested in providing a transformative educational experience. The opportunity to use interdisciplinary curriculum and project based learning was appealing to teachers as both can be culturally responsive and effective for teaching emerging multilingual students. However many teachers did not have the chance to use these approaches due to the constraints of their previous schools' instructional models and initiatives.

As leaders, we must give <u>permission</u> to change through coaching and professional development, as well as <u>compassion</u> for this major shift in teacher identity. It cannot just be lip service but true permission to mess up, change, and try something new knowing that you have their back.

Interdisciplinary Curriculum

The decision to use interdisciplinary curriculum came from the school's four core tenet process (see Chapter 1) as the group wanted students to experience the connections between subjects, project-based assessment, opportunities for real-world topics, and believed the approach would create deeper learning experiences in less time. It would have taken a curriculum design team at least four times as large to design the full curriculum from identifying the unit topic all the way to creating slide decks for every lesson. The goal for the summer was to build clear unit outlines and then provide curriculum planning time to teachers during the school year to design lessons and finish the assessments. Susan Drake's (2012) "Creating Standards-Based Integrated Curriculum: The Common Core State Standards Edition" guided the curriculum building process. The lead team followed Drake's recommendations for building interdisciplinary curriculum in three phases. Some members of the curriculum writing team were not available all summer but joined by phase:

Phase 1: Interdisciplinary Planning & Standards Placement (June–July)
Phase 2: Program Design and Considerations (late July)
Phase 3: Content Creation & Curation (early August)

Drop a marble into the jar to represent how you're entering the virtual space today!

FIGURE 3.1 Slide from summer team building activity, June 2020

Phase 1 (June into July): The 2020 summer curriculum writing began by building community and group norms as the project had unique contextual factors that most on the team were not used to: 1) very few on the team had ever developed interdisciplinary curriculum; 2) the specifics about the elementary online school were still being developed; 3) this group had a lot to accomplish in a short amount of time; and, 4) collaboration needed to happen at a distance due to the COVID-19 pandemic- a working style that was new to many at a distance, which was still new at that time. To build community and model online activities, every meeting began with a check-in to engage the group. Most meetings included a short professional development presentation on interdisciplinary curriculum or online learning, paired with an activity to practice as well as an update on the NCA school progress beyond the curriculum. The educators on the curriculum design team raised questions and concerns about NCA elementary program design that helped to refine details. Between the full-group curriculum design team meetings, grade-level teams would meet as needed with the guidance of their district lead team representative to complete that week's curriculum design activity.

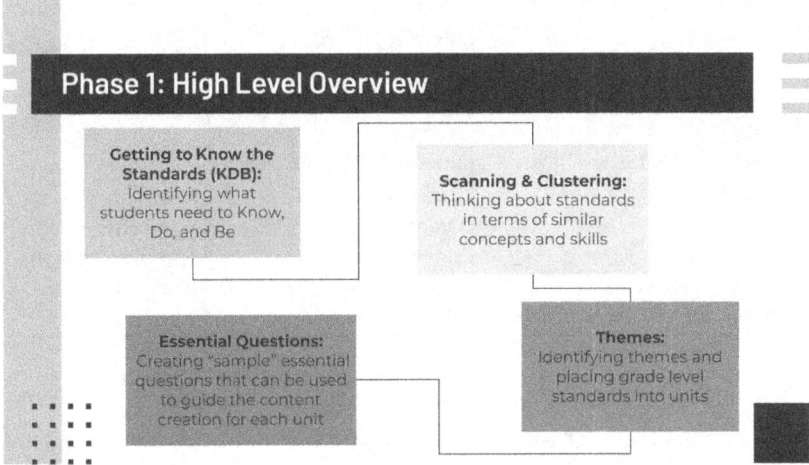

FIGURE 3.2 Slide presented to curriculum development team on phase 1 activities and plan

Source: Adapted from Drake (2012)

The first step in building the curriculum was unpacking the standards in science, math, social studies, English language arts, health, physical education, music, art, and social-emotional learning and placing them into interdisciplinary units. Each grade level group identified what students needed to know (nouns), be able to do (verbs), and be (attitudes and beliefs) within each of the standards (Drake, 2012). This process was complex for the curriculum design team as it felt like spreading tiny puzzle pieces all over a table and understanding each edge and color pattern in order to group them. Once the teachers had unpacked each standard for the know, do, and be, the lead team guided them through a series of activities to scan and cluster these skills and concepts from the standards.

TABLE 3.2 Sample Grade 2 Interdisciplinary Scan

ELA		
Disciplinary Concepts	**Interdisciplinary Concepts**	
Folktale	Cause and effect	Expression
Fables	Structure/Sequence/Order	Decode/Decompose
Story elements	Central message/moral	Patters
Text features	Challenges/concept	Questioning
Phonics/Phonemic awareness	Main idea/key details	Research
Story elements/plot	Compare/Contrast	Narrative
Mechanics/Grammar/Spelling	Comprehension	Opinion vs. fact
Handwriting	Interaction/Connection	Publish
	Poetry (beats, alliteration)	Collaboration
MATH		
Disciplinary Concepts	**Interdisciplinary Concepts**	
Algebra	Patterns	Scale
Geometry	Order	Symmetry
Measurement	Strategy	Special awareness
Numbers & operations	Quantification	Interconnections
Concrete, representational, abstract	Representation	

Following Drake's guidance, educators scanned horizontally across their grade level to identify skills and concepts that cut across the standards such as research, critical thinking, and scientific inquiry (see table 3.2). Next the educators vertically

Building the Foundation of New Learning ◆ 43

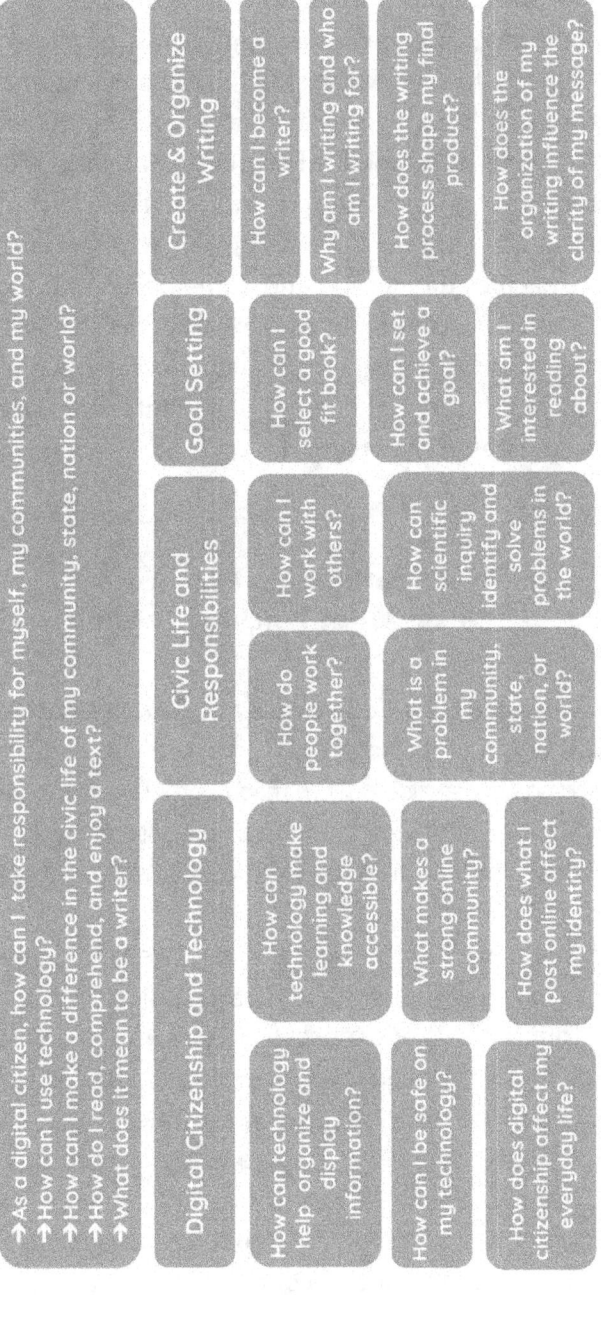

FIGURE 3.3 Example unit framework, 3rd grade

identified skills and concepts that cut across grades. This scan helped to understand if a skill or concept would be introduced for the first time and need more scaffolding, or rather if it would be appropriate to review the skill or concept within the lessons. The results of these scans were clusters of standards at each grade level that were developed into four school-wide themes broad enough to incorporate multiple subject areas. Each grade level curriculum development team developed essential questions, concept-specific mini units, and unit-specific sub-questions to guide lesson design. All unit frameworks and essential questions were reviewed for cultural inclusiveness and given feedback by the Office of Educational Equity consultants before moving onto lesson and assessment creation.

Spotlight on Practice: This Is What Teaching Is About

Kristin Bellinger, New Code Academy, Fourth Grade Teacher

It was an easy decision to join the summer curriculum writing team, as long as that didn't mean teaching online: something I'd never considered. The perks of getting paid to look at standards in a different way and teaming with district-wide leaders and teachers prompted me to sign up.

Our summer of unpacking standards reminds me of my first year of teaching—inspiring and overwhelming at the same time. I had taught fourth grade for several years and never looked at my standards on such a deep level. One of the most impactful components of the unit development was working with equity leaders and experts who challenged me to see how different questions, activities, and resources could impact various students. Although the work was challenging at times, knowing it would lead to equitable, meaningful, and authentic teaching encouraged me to take a deep breath and keep going.

Organizing the standards into four overarching K-5 themes was something that stood out to me as especially important. It provided a map for the online school to come together in meaningful and connected ways. Working with a talented and dedicated team of other fourth grade teachers and specialists from across the district was incredibly beneficial. Each of our different backgrounds, teaching styles, and ideas allowed us to craft our four units of study.

During phase two of our summer development, we began creating culminating assessments for each unit. These end of unit assessments focused on student choice, authenticity, and offered students multiple modalities. The purpose of the assessments was to offer students a sense of pride and ownership in their learning. It was during this point of the summer that I began thinking "This is what teaching is about." More importantly, this is what life is about: learning how to show what you know in a way that is unique to you while being engaged and excited about what you are creating. It was during this phase that I knew I needed to go with my gut, take a leap, and teach with the NCA.

As I began teaching online, I quickly realized that the summer curriculum we had developed needed to be looked at through a lens of flexibility. For anyone building an online school or class, it's important to anticipate shifting and rearranging within what you create. Curriculum should be designed in a way that allows teachers to have voice in the process and space for change. Our curriculum was constantly evolving to best meet the needs of our current students and make the learning as relevant and authentic as possible.

Online learning and interdisciplinary curriculum was new for both teachers and students. Although it was overwhelming to take on both at once, it also made complete sense as we were changing the way we taught from so many different angles. Interdisciplinary content allowed us to teach and model how interconnected everything truly is—both in school and in life. Online allowed so many more opportunities to make learning purposeful and engaging. Students had more time for independent work without the commotion of a traditional classroom; they were able to collaborate uninterrupted in breakout rooms with peers; and they seemed more comfortable taking chances and trying new things in the virtual space.

My year of developing interdisciplinary curriculum and teaching online was a life-changing experience. Although one of the most challenging things I've done, the work I did will stay with me and continue to evolve, which is exactly what education is meant to do.

Phase 2 (late July) introduced the curriculum planning team to frameworks and cornerstones that would drive the program-wide instructional design as the teams began building lessons for the developed units. The article "9 Ways Online Teaching Should be Different than Face-to-Face" was used as an outline for the presentation, including the recommendation that summative assessments should focus on creation (Gonzalez & Kitchen, 2020). Using the research and instructional framework, six design elements were identified that should be present in culminating assessments:

- **Authenticity:** Assessments should be relevant to students and provide opportunities for students to bring in their cultural funds of knowledge.
- **Choice:** Provide opportunities for students to choose how they will show you what they know builds autonomy and allows for students to lead with their strengths.
- **Differentiation:** Design culminating activities with the flexibility to become more or less complex based on students experiences, language proficiency, and abilities.
- **Tools of Expression:** Design activities that allow students to show what they know through multiple modalities including written, spoken, visual, and physical modes utilizing a variety of mediums.
- **Collaborative:** Designing products with peers provides opportunities for language development, critical thinking, and relationship building.

- **Assessment AS and FOR learning:** Positioning assessments as another opportunity to learn and grow gives students more ownership and acknowledges learning as a continuous process.

(CAST, 2018; DiPietro, 2010; Drake, 2012; Hammond, 2015; Kerr, 2011)

As an professional development activity, the summer curriculum design team was presented with a cluster of three second-grade standards used to design a podcasting and graphic novel culminating assessment—both projects that situate students as a creator. Next the group brainstormed creation-based culminating and interdisciplinary assessment projects, what the students would do in the projects, and what tools (both technology and not) they could use to complete the project. Ideas included creating a cheer, planning a trip, proposing a non-profit organization, building a website, designing a movie trailer, developing a wax museum, building a Rube Goldberg machine, and performing a puppet show. The brainstormed list was shared with the curriculum design team as they developed culminating assessments using the unit framework and standards for students to answer the unit's essential question through a performance task. The NCA teachers finished designing the culminating projects with accompanying student-centered rubrics, which ultimately served as assessment *as* learning as well as a celebration of their work.

Phase 3 (Early August) was focused on designing the first 20 days of school. It is customary for brick-and-mortar schools to focus on building routines, relationships, and classroom management norms the first few weeks of school. In online school, there is the added twist of helping students become online learners, which includes understanding how to use the core tools and building independent learning skills. As this process is so essential, all of chapter five is devoted to what this looks like in detail.

> **Spotlight on Practice: Building Interdisciplinary Curriculum Provides a High Return on Investment**

Colleen Gunkel, New Code Academy, Fifth Grade Teacher

It was always a dream to teach interdisciplinary after learning about it in my Master's program because the approach increased engagement and provided opportunities to be culturally relevant and responsive. Ultimately, the interdisciplinary curriculum that we built and used provided more time for students to focus on engaging projects, new opportunities for assessment, and an evolving curriculum that keeps the content relevant for students. Designing the curriculum was a lot of work on the front end: analyzing standards, reviewing resources, and considering a range of ways assessments that align with our objectives. However, this investment in time to connect multiple subjects saved us a lot of time in the classroom. Instead of planning for several different buckets of time during the day we used a longer interdisciplinary block to dive in deeper. The students had fun creating projects and seemed more engaged than anything I had done before teaching 5th grade in person.

One project that sticks out to me was our Unit 3 curriculum that covers European colonists, Native American Tribes, and the Revolutionary War. Our English language arts standards include persuasive writing so for one assignment we had the student pick a role within the Revolutionary War and write a letter as a patriot or a loyalist. For the final project, students could work independently or with a partner and choose a writing prompt such as debating between a patriot or loyalist perspective, or an interview with a colonist. They dressed up and got really into character and recorded their projects using WeVideo. It required them to know the content from a variety of perspectives, and it was much more engaging than an informational report. Additionally, they had fun watching their peers' work which was another opportunity to experience the content.

Building the units ourselves and having support from the social justice team also ensured we included resources that examined this time period from multiple perspectives. Our district's curriculum primarily teaches this time period from the perspective of the founding father and other white men. In our book clubs we chose novels that examined the experience and perspective of women, people who were enslaved, and Native Americans. One thing to plan for when adopting an interdisciplinary curriculum is that it will be everchanging. As state standards and district curriculum are cyclically revised and updated, or if you are co-teaching with a new colleague, there will need to be updates. This is not a big deal, however, as this work would naturally happen even if you didn't adopt an interdisciplinary curriculum, and as a designer of the curriculum, I can see connections for new standards much easier now.

Building in Parallel

While the curriculum was being built, the digital learning team was busy turning the concept of an online school into a reality including solidifying Washburn Elementary—a brick-and-mortar school in the district—as the NCA partner school. This provided a physical location to store and pick up material resources, where teachers could work if they needed to go into a building, and share administrative staff. The NCA classroom teacher job posting became available for internal applicants in July, and the leadership team was looking for applicants that had shown leadership in educational technology, committed to equity, and had demonstrated the ability to try new things. The UofM research-practice partners provided a resource to guide the development of interview questions, including asking candidates about their ability to foster strong relationships with parents and guardians, motivate students from a distance, and evidence of their communication and technological skills (DiPietro, 2010). The interest for these positions were high as the job descriptions were posted as "teacher on special assignment" roles which guaranteed teachers their previous building, grade, and class in the district after two years. Initially, NCA hired for two sections per grade but increased to three sections in most grades by the end of August which, unfortunately, sent district brick-and-mortar principals racing to find longer-term substitute teachers for their roles.

While hiring for NCA elementary was taking place, the fully online school option was being communicated to in-district families. August was filled with virtual family information sessions on the details of the NCA model and enrollment process. If families opted into NCA, they were agreeing to stay in the program all year—no switching between online school and brick-and-mortar school. These information sessions stressed that NCA was not emergency remote teaching but an intentionally designed online school. Contextually, schools around the country were gearing up for another year of unknown with new COVID-19 mitigation strategies including masks and ventilation; the arrival date of vaccines for adults was still unknown. This likely drove more families to enroll in NCA, and enrollment rates were growing through September. Enrollment took place through an interdistrict transfer process with no cutoff date. Once sections were full, waitlists were created at grade levels. The digital learning team was hurriedly ordering materials and preparing technology for teachers and students.

The summer of 2020 was an exciting moment of problem solving and program development; however, every team and project mentioned in this chapter would have benefitted from more time. What did not get done in the curriculum building process ultimately fell to NCA teachers in the first year of online teaching, which became a professional and personal strain for many (see Chapter 5). However, district-created online curriculum resulted in teachers having more autonomy and made the content more relevant for students. Those on the summer curriculum development team have shared that the summer development time served as a form of professional learning as they thought deeply about standards, assessments, and equity strategies in a way they might not have if a curriculum had been assigned to them. Ultimately the interdisciplinary curriculum that has been designed is dynamic and engaging for students and a true point of pride for NCA teachers.

Some Questions to Consider as a Team or Individually When Building the Program:
- What are the core tenets of your program and how does that shape your curriculum needs?
- What are all the school components that need to be built, and who is in charge of the process?
- What are the short-term and long-term costs associated with different program and curricula models?
- What should the student experience be and how does that impact curriculum selection?
- What professional development or team building might a group who does not regularly work together need for a special project?

References

CAST. (2018). *Universal design for learning guidelines version 2.2.* http://udlguidelines.cast.org

Dipietro, M. (2010). Virtual school pedagogy: The instructional practices of K-12 virtual school teachers. *Journal of Educational Computing Research, 42*(3), 327–354.

Drake, S. M. (2012). *Creating standards-based integrated curriculum: The common core state standards edition.* Corwin Press.

Gonzalez, J., & Kitchen, M. (2020, July 5). *9 ways online teaching should be different than face-to-face.* Cult of Pedagogy. https://www.cultofpedagogy.com/9-ways-online-teaching/

Hammond, Z. (2015). *Culturally responsive teaching and the brain: Promoting authentic engagement and rigor among culturally and linguistically diverse students.* Corwin Press.

Kerr, S. (2011). Tips, tools, and techniques for teaching in the online high school classroom. *TechTrends, 55*(1), 28–31.

4

Designing an Elementary Online Program

The following chapter will overview the multitude of elementary online program design elements, of which the student schedule is the most requested by families and peer schools. The design of New Code Academy Elementary is a manifestation of the school's core tenets, the commitment to equity as shared in previous chapters, the work of district educators and instructional leaders, and feedback from students and families. There is a wide variety of online elementary school models, and currently no substantial research on the effects of different approaches schools take. The NCA model in this chapter is one approach to elementary online learning that the school community is proud of and can confidently assert provides students with a high quality learning environment.

Program Design Development

In the summer of 2020, families who had identified they would be sending their children to NCA were engaged in a series of feedback sessions. The most commonly asked question at the elementary level was related to how much screen time would be required to participate in NCA. This concern of parents and teachers was addressed by intentionally including a balance of on and off screen time when planning the schedule and expectations. The second most common question was if the needs of students with Individual Education Plans (IEPs) could be met online. NCA's special education lead set up follow-up meetings with each family to talk through their child's specific needs. In addition to feedback from families, teachers in the curriculum development team asked questions about the program that helped leadership work out some of the details that had not been considered such as: will there be training available for families that opt into this program? Will families understand that they are signing up for a more rigorous online experience than emergency remote learning? How will primary students get hands-on materials that are needed for school? The feedback and questions from the various groups helped move the planning process from a 10,000-foot view closer to the ground.

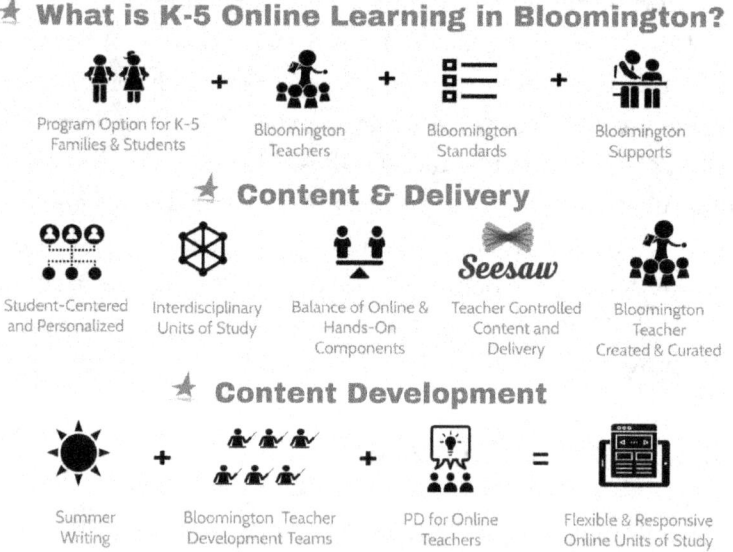

FIGURE 4.1 K-5 program design model communicated in summer 2020 to potential families

What resulted from the early feedback from families, the core school tenets developed in the spring prior, and insights from the summer curriculum design team was the school model in the image above. This infographic was used in family communication when NCA began enrolling district students. Notably, this early framing communicated the school would be Bloomington-based, intentionally designed, and that instruction would be responsive to student needs. NCA's program model consists of four interconnected categories of design elements represented in NCA elementary school's model: brain-based learning, structure, staffing, and resources.

Brain-Based Learning

The design of academic instruction was grounded in discussions of what elementary bodies and minds need to learn. In addition to the use of brain-based instructional strategies including culturally responsive teaching and Universal Design for Learning (Chapter 1), as well as standards-based interdisciplinary curriculum (Chapter 3), the NCA program prioritizes whole body learning through physical materials and brain breaks.

Hands-on by Design
It is well established that physical materials and manipulatives help with motor development, create engagement, and make abstract concepts more concrete. Paper and pencil is the most common physical material NCA uses as elementary students need to learn how to physically write and the process helps with reading and letter perception. Paper and pencil might seem odd to point out but in some online elementary programs, work is done entirely through the computer. The use of physical manipulatives and activities through Play-Doh, dice, and popsicle sticks can create balance between modalities that will also limit screen time and promote independent practice. In a live lesson, a class will get out the same materials together so the teacher

can model using a ten-block or cutting with a pair of scissors. During an independent practice, this could be as simple as a student handwriting in their journal or building a pattern from found objects in their house, and then uploading a picture of either to the learning management system. The use of materials has perplexed a few parents in the past who see how much more efficiently lessons can be done if all done completely digital; but, brain and development research as well as the experience of NCA educators indicates the use of physical materials is important.

Rebalancing the Brain Though Breaks

Throughout these instructional opportunities are consistent brain breaks. These moments to pause actually help the brain make connections while resting, resulting in more productivity, creativity, and ability to socialize (Immordino-Yang et al., 2012). Hammond (2015) also stresses the importance of teaching small chunks of information paired with unstructured think time as the human brain will tune out and essentially go on break if you do not provide one during class. Given the lack of physical transitions students would experience in brick-and-mortar

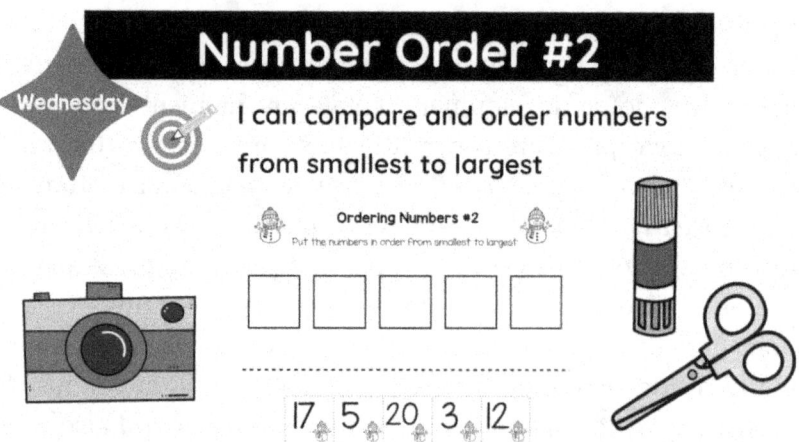

FIGURE 4.2 Kindergarten Seesaw assignment: Ordering numbers with cut out cards

class, NCA teachers opt for movement breaks that often involve dancing with music or playing a game like Simon says. All live classroom meetings that are more than 15 minutes include at least one brain break. In addition to brain breaks, NCA has a one-hour lunch and movement break where students are encouraged to go screen-free and get outside. Families with multiple children in NCA elementary and/or an adult who takes their lunch break at the same time helps in getting kids active and playing during lunch. Families were given these active play ideas for lunch and movement breaks:

Active Play Ideas	
Indoor Activities	**Outdoor Activities**
Dance to Baby Shark Mindful stretching Jumping jacks Do push ups Couch cushion obstacle course Run in place Dance to Thriller Blanket fort	Play in the snow Run around your house or building Use signs to find wildlife Bounce a ball Build in the snow Go for a 5-minute walk Bike for 5 minutes Get the mail

Curriculum

NCA's interdisciplinary curriculum (see Chapter 3) has become a hallmark element of the program as it allows students to learn standards in an integrated way and transfer learning concepts across disciplines/subject areas. Student creation, identities, and choice are prioritized as teachers design lessons and project options for each unit.

Community Building and Social Emotional Instruction

It is imperative that students and families feel included in their class and the greater school community as a whole. To ensure this happens, 45 minutes a day is dedicated to building belongingness through morning meetings and closing circles as well as ensuring teachers have appropriate class sizes. Relationships are at the core of NCA's model both between students with their teachers, and students with their peers. To read more information about intentional community building, see Chapter 10.

Structure

Students and their families benefit from a consistent and predictable schedule and routine. Students are able to focus their attention on academics and participating when the schedule is familiar. Learning coaches, many of whom are working their jobs from home, are also able to find a rhythm and more easily monitor that their child is following the schedule when the structure is dependable.

Schedule

NCA has a base schedule with consistent whole school components with teacher-led adaptations at the lower-(K–2) and upper-elementary (3–5) level:

- **Morning meeting**: Every student's day begins with a morning meeting that is focused on building community, social-emotional learning, and grounds the student in the day. Chapter 6 details community building within the morning meeting in more detail.
- **Live whole and small group instruction:** Each student has one block of math and one block of interdisciplinary instruction that begins with a whole group lesson and transitions into small group instruction (see Chapter 7). While students are not in small groups, they work on independent learning activities housed within Seesaw (see Chapter 8).
- **Specialist:** Each class participates in one specialist (music, physical education, and art) lesson per day with live and independent activity elements. Bi-monthly computer science was added for the 2021–2022 school year.

- **Closing circle:** Every day ends with a closing circle to celebrate the day and reflect on shared experiences. As students are in different physical spaces and do not have as many shared daily experiences such as eating the same lunch or reacting to a fire drill, the closing circle provides an opportunity to connect as a group before transitioning out of a student role for the day.
- **Flex time:** At the end of the day there is about 30 minutes of flexible time that teachers use differently based on their style and student needs. Some use it for structured 1:1 meetings, others use it for open teacher hours, and some lead activities for students to connect socially.

On Wednesdays, NCA has a modified schedule to provide teachers with time to prepare live and independent interdisciplinary learning activities, give students detailed feedback, identify differentiated instructional needs, organize monthly material pick up, update asset-based learning profiles, and co-plan with colleagues. This modified day originated from district brick-and-mortar schools that were experiencing different formats of emergency remote teaching, and the NCA school recognized online teachers needed a similar schedule. Stressed throughout this book is the concept that time in online learning looks different and requires a different schedule than brick-and-mortar classrooms. The modified schedules provide students a day to continue learning at their own pace, make choices in their learning, catch up on assignments if needed, and extend their learning in different ways.

At the end of year one, it was determined that there was too much variety in how teachers were structuring their Wednesdays with students, and this was hard for families with multiple students in the school. For the 2021–2022 school year, added to Wednesdays were brick-and-mortar makerspace, book checkout, and storytime sessions with NCA's media director as well as virtual clubs and enrichment computer science lessons. School-wide

TABLE 4.1 Third Grade Student Example Schedule for Monday, Tuesday, Thursday, and Friday

Time	Activity	
9:00–9:30	**Morning Meeting** • Greeting/Share • Game • Brain break (video or song)	
9:30–10:00	**Block 1 Whole Group –** *Math* • Math talk/warm up problem • Math lesson	
10:05–10:20	**Small Group 1** • Review/reteach • Differentiated content • Practice	**If not in small group:** Independent math work
10:25–10:40	**Small Group 2**	
10:45–11:00	**Read Aloud** • Read from a chapter book as students have snack/quiet time.	
11:00–11:45 (teacher prep)	**Live specialist lesson:** • A Day: Music • B Day: P.E. • C Day: Art	
11:45–12:45	**Lunch & Active Brain Break**	
12:45–1:45	Block 2 Whole Group: ELA – Science – Social Studies interdisciplinary • Read aloud • Lesson	
1:20–1:35	**Small Group 1** • Guided reading rotation	**If not in small group:** Independent reading work
1:40–1:55	**Small Group 2**	
2:00–2:15	**Small Group 3**	
2:20–2:35	**Small Group 4**	
2:45–3:00	**Whole Group Closing Meeting** • Review work that was sent out for the day and what needs to be finished during study hall • Play a game	
3:00–3:30	**1:1 Check-ins**	**If not in 1:1 check-ins:** Study hall

office hours have been added at 10:30 each Wednesday so families can get any questions they have answered. This change created more consistency across the program and simplified what families needed to know.

TABLE 4.2 Example Student Schedule for Wednesdays 2021–2022

9:00–9:30	**Morning Meeting With Class** • Wonderful Wednesday NewsBYTEs with overview of asynchronous afternoon offerings • Greeting/Share • Game/Activity • Brain break (Video or Song)	
9:30–10:30	**Whole Group Activities** • Lesson • Collaborative work time • Show asynchronous work and give directions for the afternoon	
10:30–10:45	**Family Office Hours** • Families can join the meeting to ask questions about the afternoon learning activities or asynchronous offerings	
10:45–11:45	**Independent Work Time** • Complete asynchronous teacher assignments on Seesaw • Catch up and enrichment options	
11:45–12:45	**Lunch and Movement Break**	**Teacher Preparation Time**
12:45–3:20	**Seesaw Specialist Activity** • Independent activity assigned by art, music, physical education, or computer science specialist **Virtual Specialist Clubs** • Optional live clubs led by a specialist teacher **Brick-and-Mortar Partner School Offerings** • Makerspace with NCA tech integrationist • Media lessons with NCA media specialist • Book check-out in the media center	• Lesson and curriculum design • Review student work and provide feedback • Grading • Co-planning meetings • Professional development

Communication

A key to providing structure and dependable routines to students and families is consistent and clear communication. This includes providing clarity around the program design and expectations *before* families register, as well as regular communication from the school and teacher on what is happening next, and taking time to celebrate together. Chapter 9 describes the home-to-school

Wednesday, December 15 en español

VIRTUAL OPTIONS *optional			IN PERSON OPTIONS 8401 Xerxes Ave S, Bloomington, MN 55431 *please park in the front of the building		
1:30-2:15 **Grade 4** Virtual Art with Ms. Krueger Meet Link	1:30-2:15 **Grade 2** Virtual Phy Ed with Ms. Blasingame Meet Link	1:30-2:15 **Grade K** Virtual Music with Mrs. Yurecko Meet Link	Media Lesson with Mrs. Lambrecht All NCA elementary students are welcome at any of the lessons! 11:45-12:05 1:30-1:50 2:30-2:50	Library Check Out Library check-out is open from: 10:45-12:15 1:00-3:00	Makerspace with Mr. Cannon Come explore and create with Mr. Cannon in the NCA makerspace. 10:45-2:00
2:15-3:00 **Grade 5** Virtual Art with Ms. Krueger Meet Link	2:15-3:00 **Grade 3** Virtual Phy Ed with Ms. Blasingame Meet Link	2:15-3:00 **Grade 1** Virtual Music with Mrs. Yurecko Meet Link			

FIGURE 4.4 Modified Wednesday afternoon options shared with families

connection including communication in detail. As it pertains to program design, do not underestimate the time and coordination it takes to pull all these details together, create media that families can utilize, and translate communication into home languages. A weekly "New Code Newsflash" is sent out to all families and translated into Spanish and Somali. It includes a weekly message, important dates, school events (e.g. spirit week), latest resources from the family education committee, school NewsBYTEs show, and program-wide static information such as phone numbers and resources. It is sent through email, Seesaw, and Remind text message.

Additionally, teachers were provided with a template to give families with a "Peek at the Week" and a script that encouraged concise and simple language in the accompanied message.

Staffing and Leadership

Online students need and deserve the same access to licensed staff and specialists that brick-and-mortar students need. If leaders plan an online school with a staffing model that is less than

Designing an Elementary Online Program ◆ 63

A Peek at the Week: November 8-12

What are we learning this week?

Theme	Literacy	Math	Daily Schedule
Friendship	Reading Stations Sight Words - **go** **to** Letter Features Beginning Sounds (recognize and label) Writing a simple sentence.	Counting On From 5	9:00 - Morning Meeting 9:45 - Reading Rotations 10:30 - Play Break 11:00 - Read Aloud 12:45 - Specialists 1:45 - Quiet Time/Math 3:00 - Closing Meeting

Daily Notes:

Monday	Tuesday	Wednesday	Thursday	Friday
QOTD Read the numbers. 8 3 5 7 12 16 19 14 Evening Task Watch Alphabet Chant Play a Math Game	QOTD Show me the chants for these words: **go** **to** Evening Task Play a Literacy Game	*Wednesday Schedule* QOTD What sound do you hear at the beginning of: Evening Task Watch Alphabet Chant	QOTD Tell about the features of these letters: S M K P r g a l Evening Task Play a Math Game Read "Places We Go"	QOTD How many? Count on from 5. Evening Task Read "Family Fun" Check Seesaw

FIGURE 4.5 Kindergarten peek at the week using NCA provided template

what is provided in physical school buildings, the results will be just that: less than. For instance, several students have transferred in from other programs—particularly from online for-profit charter schools—where they would be in a live class meeting with over 100 students and never had the opportunity to build relationships with their teacher or peers. Like any school, the staffing model at NCA is not perfect and could always benefit from more caring adults to teach and support students. Fluctuations in staffing between year one and year two were a result of student enrollment (350 students in 2020–21 and 200 in 2021–22) and student academic needs. However, the size of the district and the number of families who opted into NCA in its first year provided an opportunity to launch with a substantial sized staff.

Spotlight on Practice: Online Physical Education Builds Real-life Fitness and Health

Janelle Berry-Blasingame, New Code Academy, K-5 Physical Education Specialist

During the pandemic, online physical education (PE) became a target for internet jokes and criticism as people couldn't imagine kids working out through a computer. Our society has such a strong mental image of "gym class" in a giant gym with shiny wood floors. Traditional PE classes, in which working out is organized around a large group of people in a large gym forced to play the same sport, is not representative of what fitness looks like after high school. Online PE teaches body movements that can be applied to different physical activities and models for students how to use items in their home environment to stay active.

My lessons are 45 minutes long and begin with team building, as most sports are team or social activities. We do group stretching and warm-up activities before a skill demonstration. Some skill demonstrations happen live so I can give feedback on student form before they practice independently. Other skill demonstrations are recorded for students to watch if the activity doesn't work well in a live video meeting.

Students are only required to submit a video demonstrating the skill if it is being assessed. When I first started teaching online, I had students submit videos of their daily practice, and I'd watch every video and send feedback. The amount of time to create those videos became impossible to keep up with, and the kids seemed to be spending a lot of time on Seesaw rather than moving their bodies. I depend on the relationships I build with my students and the support from their parents to ensure they are practicing. There might be independent activities students choose not to participate in or try their best at, but that also happens every day in brick-and-mortar PE.

Engaging in movement together through a class meeting allows for more immediate feedback and reduces the constant comparison of performance between kids. I changed the settings in our video call to "presenter mode" so that kids see a big video of me versus their peers. This encourages kids to try their best and can reduce the embarrassment some students experience when they have to be physically active around their peers.

Elementary PE is all about skill building, specifically locomotor skills in grades K-2. This includes learning the vocabulary and practicing bending, swaying, twisting, and jumping. The goal is to give students opportunities to develop and practice moving their body safely from one place to another while staying healthy. Some students may use PE skills—squats for example, on a future softball team as they field the ball; others might practice squats to stay healthy, and some might just be more aware of their body while squatting to reach and lift something.

I get to demonstrate real-life fitness and show kids that you don't need expensive gym equipment to be physically active. Sometimes mishaps happen on screen as my ball goes flying or my cat joins in during stretching; it is all very fun. We adapt what materials we can to teach the skills; for instance we provide plastic cups and a rubber ball for bowling. Kids are thinking outside of the box and finding physical movement that they enjoy doing at home.

Partner School

NCA utilizes a partner school model with Washburn Elementary, a district brick-and-mortar elementary, to create consistency in where overlapping services would originate from. This partnership creates a central place for material prep and pick up, access to the media center and library books, and storage space. As this was a new concept for both schools, there was ultimately some confusion in how a brick-and-mortar school and online school "partner." After the first school year, staff from both schools met to define the partnership as "a mutually supportive relationship between Washburn and NCA in which the partners commit themselves to specific goals and activities intended to benefit all students and staff." As well as identified norms in how to work together by being flexible, sharing and creating a welcoming space, seek understanding rather than assuming, showing empathy for colleagues.

Instructional Staff

The staffing model at NCA includes:

- **Classroom teachers:** Three classroom teachers per grade level K-5 with no more than 29 students per class in 2020–2021 school year. Each grade was reduced to two sections for the 2021–2022 school year.
- **Specialists:** There were three full-time specialists for music, art, and physical education for the 2020–2021 school year, and a computer science specialist was added for the 2021–2022 school year. Each class has a specialist content live lesson once a day and a computer science live lesson twice a month. In addition to teaching live lessons, these specialists also serve as push-in support for students during independent work time. Additionally, NCA hired a half-time reading specialist for year two as the student need justified the additional capacity.

- **Special Education and English language teachers:** Both years there was one English language teacher who supports 40 students. In 2020–2021 there were two special education teachers and one for the 2021–2022 school year. Additionally, there are three paraprofessionals that supported special education.
- **Split modality staff:** In addition to the staff listed who worked 100% with NCA students, there were also staff from across the district who split their time between brick-and-mortar schools and NCA including an equity specialist, developmental adapted physical education specialists, nurse, reading specialist (year 1), social workers, speech therapists, occupational therapists, and administrative clerk. Many of these professionals regularly split their time between multiple buildings. The partner school is a smaller district elementary so combined with NCA, the total students many of these split modality staff serve is similar to that of other district elementary schools.
- **Technology integration specialist:** There is one full-time technology integration specialist who works across K-8 NCA.

Find Program Champions

The concept of a technology integrationist specialist might seem strange for a fully online school, but the role and the dynamic human in that role proved to be essential. One of New Code Academy's champions is Ray Cannon, a passionate and creative leader with a background in music education. To fund his position initially, Ray served as half-time K-8 tech integration and half-time online middle school music, which allowed him to see the program from various perspectives to identify problems and create solutions. His solutions included family technology sessions that build comfort with the technology and introduce him as a resource so that families can get in-the-moment troubleshooting support for any issues they might be having. To build community, he launched a school-wide news show that has become the highlight of students' week (see Chapter 10). He ensures teachers know about and are able to use new features in technology platforms and provides pedagogical ideas. He also has developed a catalog of family tech tip videos on digital competency and safety.

It is important to highlight Ray's work within the staffing section because it is not about the positions; it is about the people. As schools and districts invest in building and growing online schools, finding passionate and talented program champions like Ray is essential and worth creative budgeting. There are many anecdotal stories from other districts in which the online program leadership was added to someone's plate who already had a full time role and/or does not have a passion for launching an online program. Seek out champions—as NCA did—who believe in the possibility of online learning and are willing to contribute their time and talents to making the school the best it can be for students.

Leadership Model

The non-traditional leadership model is informed by a series of contextual factors that were present when the school was being launched and budget factors that dictate administrative capacity. NCA elementary is led by a district Digital Learning Coordinator responsible for program development, curriculum, outreach, communication, budget management, teacher professional development and support, staff meetings, and material coordination. As the first point person, the Digital Learning Coordinator triages which school or district leadership administrator a question or an issue should include. The NCA assistant principal supports the K-12 online program with learning supports, relationship-based problem solving through the individual student support team (ISST) related to academic, social-emotional and attendance concerns, teacher supervision, budget management, and program development at the online middle and high school. The school principal who is also the administrator for the partner school is responsible for NCA staffing, human resource components, and meetings with parents and students. Additionally, the school had deep engagement and support from district leaders representing curriculum and instruction, special education, English language learning, and gifted and talented departments.

Partnering and Program Evaluation

Early in the school design, Bloomington Public Schools partnered with the Learning + Technologies Collaborative at the University of Minnesota. This research-practice partnership provides the staff and leaders with the latest insights about online pedagogy, input on decisions and designs from outside experts, and professional development support. NCA's university partners lead program evaluation throughout the year with parents, students, and teachers, and findings are used to develop new resources, training, and adjustments to the program design.

Resources

The online modality requires learning devices and platforms, and the NCA brain-based instructional framework prioritizes the use of physical materials and manipulatives for elementary learners. Whenever possible, students having the same resources makes instruction efficient and more equitable. Equity also means that students have access to basic resources including food, clothing, and additional supplies (see Chapter 2). Providing all of these resources requires a significant amount of coordination and involvement of different staff and district services but is essential in supporting the school's core tenets and beliefs.

Materials

Providing educational materials is one of the heaviest lifts of the program. NCA students purchase or are provided standard school supplies such as crayons, notebooks, and erasers like most brick-and-mortar students. Materials are everything that a brick-and-mortar school provides beyond school supplies to students within the classroom environment such as workbooks, math manipulatives, individual whiteboards and markers, dice, decks of cards, and popsicle sticks. These are items that students generally use for an activity or unit and then get stored away in the classroom until the next year.

Example kindergarten material, 2020:

- Binders
- Laminating sheets
- Chart paper (big)
- Chart paper (small)
- Whiteboards
- Sheet protectors
- Disc counters
- Birthday pencils
- Magnets for magnetic letters
- Wiki stix
- Pipe cleaners
- Pony beads
- Craft sticks
- Chalk
- Colored craft sticks
- Mini ziplock baggies
- Erasers
- Two-color counters
- Bingo chips
- Baking sheets
- Foam dice
- Playing cards
- Pom poms
- Play-Doh

In the summer, each teacher was given a budget of $400 for hands-on learning materials which was purchased by the administrative clerk. Developmentally, more materials were needed at the younger grades. Once a month, material pick-up day is hosted where a paper bag of academic items that are organized by the teachers is distributed to the students in a drive-up fashion and delivered to families that are not available during pick-up times. In the 2021–2022 school year, NCA began enrolling students from outside of the district requiring some student materials to be shipped. The teachers are in charge of coordinating with their grade-level peers, sending documents for copying to the administrative clerk a week prior, and putting the materials in each bag. The pick-up days require a lot of logistical planning and communication, and NCA's administrative clerk developed and leads the process which has become smoother over time.

> **Spotlight on Practice: Using Materials to Move From Concrete to Abstract Online**

Rachel Mersch, New Code Academy, Kindergarten Teacher

We know that being able to touch, manipulate, and count materials in elementary classrooms is critical. This is true whether borrowing numbers or counting to five. As the online program was in development, my teaching partner and I made the case to leaders for a material budget and distribution plan. We were provided $400 a classroom which allowed us to buy uniform materials that come in the same packaging for each student. When students have access to the same learning materials at the same time it feels more like a classroom experience. The screen becomes the method for which they are hearing you but they are still doing all the same things in front of them.

My teammate and I can be type A in how we package, send home, and share information with parents, but the time we invest in organizing we get back in smooth transitions when teaching. Whenever there is material pickup or delivery, we take a picture of all the items within Seesaw and add labels about what the item is and how we will use it: here is the gym ball they will need for specialists; this learning packet is for week x, and please add this page to your Megabyte binder. We also send home a weekly email calendar that indicates the materials they will need by day and by hour. Kindergarteners do not have the executive functioning skills to organize their materials without guidance, but we do encourage families to involve their children in preparing their materials for the next day. This builds independent learning skills and makes for a less stressful day for students and their learning coach.

Our essential materials that we use often are:

- The students' "Megabyte Binder," a three-ring binder that holds reference materials like a word wall, alphabet chart, generic game map, and letter caterpillar.
- Paper learning packets that we designed to support the messages and learning objectives for every day. These include literacy games, site word practice, letter of the day, and morning messages that I have written on the board behind me when I teach so that students can circle site words in front of them.
- All NCA students have the same Sterilite bin to house their materials at home. It keeps things simple and uniform. Within it, we pack counting chips and dice for math and literacy games, whiteboard and marker for students to practice and show, and Play-Doh to make letters, numbers, and shapes.
- We do a lot of arts and crafts in kindergarten, both as an extension of our learning standards and because students need to build their fine motor skills. Supplies needed for this include crayons, glue, construction paper, scissors, cotton balls, pipe cleaners, etc.
- The use of all the materials above are supported by the use of my document camera. As we play games, count, roll, and write, the students can use their manipulatives in front of them while I model and direct with the camera.

The preparation and use of these materials is essential for us to teach kindergarten. I couldn't do it any other way. Parents have shared that the information and organization we send home is a lifesaver and allows their child to take ownership of their learning.

One material oversight of year one was underestimating the need for books when building the materials budget. Although teachers were willing to share their own "at-home" classroom libraries with students, there was a dire need for books for classroom read-alouds and student independent reading. To remedy this, each team was provided with $500–$1000 to order books for their classroom libraries, teacher libraries, and for guided reading or book clubs. In year two, book costs were included in the budget. There was an estimated cost savings of 8–12% in running an online school compared to other district brick-and-mortar elementary schools; particularly related to food service, custodial services, facilities and transportation. However, there were additional expenses related to materials, shipping, assessment adjustments (e.g. outstate testing centers) and technology.

Technology

The district already had strong technology integration practices and systems with educational access to hardware and software built prior to designing NCA. This foundation made the program design related to technology easier. For hardware, all students were given a touchscreen tablet at grades K-1 and a touchscreen Chromebook at grades 2–5. In year two, all students switched to touchscreen Chromebooks as the device performed better in terms of connection and processing. Seesaw serves as NCA's learning management system, communication tool, and independent lesson design platform. Seesaw is currently the best tool on the market for elementary brick-and-mortar and online learning because it focuses on student creation (not consumption) and is designed in a way that is elementary friendly. The navigation throughout the platform is intuitive and does not require users to know how to read, which is essential for elementary learners. More about how Seesaw is used for lessons, feedback, and independent learning in Chapter 8.

Google is the district-wide productivity suite as it is the best option on the market currently for a K-12 environment.

NCA elementary utilizes Google Drive for digital file storage; Google meets, for live instruction and Google Slides for visuals in all live meetings. Collaboration takes place with Google Documents and the whiteboard tool, Jamboard. Polls are created in Google Meet, and Google Forms are used for formative assessments. All students and staff also have access to Gmail for their email and chat but this is utilized more in the upper elementary. Staff also use Gmail to contact parents as well as Remind, a tool that provides text messaging without exchanging phone numbers.

Food

In addition to materials and technology, some families depend on schools to support basic needs. Families can pick up or have meal kits delivered if they live within the district or a close suburb. This service was going to conclude after year one as the district was no longer preparing meal kits for emergency distance learning. NCA staff and leaders advocated that food continue to be available in year two and were successful in convincing the district. Additionally, families can come to one of the district's high schools each week and pick up food and groceries through a district program. A current limitation of the program is getting food to families that live farther away. The NCA social worker has connected families to food banks but not prepared daily meals.

Families have left other online and brick-and-mortar schools to join NCA because the program model aligns with the needs of their child and the values of the family. There have also been families that opt-out of NCA to go back to the brick-and-mortar classroom at the end of the year. In the feedback collected from surveys, emails, and phone calls from families, the praises for the program design and teachers outweigh complaints and criticisms. Online learning is a choice program that is preferred by some students, while some families are choosing this option because of the pandemic. There are different models based on the elements above that schools can design and families can select based on the needs of their students.

Questions to Consider When Building Your Model:
- What are the ways in which learning happens, and how does that shape your program model?
- How does your program model align with the latest research on learning, cognition, and child development?
- How much synchronous time is right for your program, if any?
- What will your attendance and work completion policies look like?
- What materials do your students need and what systems can be developed to support the delivery?
- Time within online learning is different from brick-and-mortar schooling. How will your schedule accommodate the additional time teachers need to prepare, build, and give feedback?
- What are the non-negotiables for a school within your district system?
- How will you staff your school with a principal, secretary, nurse, support staff, etc.?

References

Hammond, Z. (2015). *Culturally responsive teaching and the brain: Promoting authentic engagement and rigor among culturally and linguistically diverse students.* Corwin Press.

Immordino-Yang, M. H., Christodoulou, J. A., & Singh, V. (2012). Rest is not idleness: Implications of the brain's default mode for human development and education. *Perspectives on Psychological Science, 7*(4), 352–364.

5

Facilitating Teacher Professional Development

The following chapter will detail the professional development led with staff who had no formal experience in online learning prior to becoming a New Code Academy teacher. The transition from brick-and-mortar to virtual teaching was supported by back-to-school workshops and resources, grade-level coaching, and collegial sharing and reflection opportunities.

These online teaching positions were highly competitive and allowed NCA to recruit some of the most talented educators from across the district for its first year as a school. Almost all of the hired NCA teachers were tenured professionals who had been working within education for 5+ years, and all knew their standards and were adept at effective teaching strategies. Due to the lack of information and experience about elementary online schooling, it was a challenge for instructional leaders to plan how best to support this group of teachers in their new role. The smallest teacher moves, such as looking over a student's shoulder to see their work, to the deep-rooted pedagogical identities that this group of educators had spent years developing, were challenged throughout the first

DOI: 10.4324/9781003281498-5

year of online teaching. The staff quickly found that strategies and approaches that work in brick-and-mortar classrooms do not always translate to the online modality. At the end of their first year (spring 2021), during teacher reflective focus groups New Code Academy elementary teachers described the year as a "learning curve," "completely different," and "building the airplane while you fly it."

Spotlight on Practice: Embrace the Change of Teaching Online

Gina Schroeder, New Code Academy, First Grade Teacher

I had taught in the brick-and-mortar classroom for 14 years before teaching online at NCA. I considered myself to be flexible and open minded to new ideas and strategies professionally and becoming an online teacher put those two traits to the test. My new colleagues and I were trying to figure out how to deliver this content that we've delivered for years in our craft differently, how to reach our students and families in a different way, and send out material in a different way. There was so much for us to figure out all at once. We didn't know how to be an online teacher, and our students didn't know how to be online learners; yet together we figured it out.

The most challenging element to being an online teacher is the lack of control. As a first grade teacher I was used to physically helping students who were struggling to write a letter, or cut a paper, or find their materials. If students learning at home couldn't find their Play-Doh or pencil for the activity, I couldn't hand them another through the screen. I couldn't provide hands-on support when students were struggling with an assignment on paper or in Seesaw. Sometimes this led to frustration for both myself and the students as I would coach them to take a deep breath, try again, and watch me one more time. My students and I overcame a lot of these challenges with unique ways of sharing the work through the camera and a lot of communication.

To help with the lost materials and tools, we worked together to build systems of organization such as turning material preparation into a game so they would be ready for the rest of the day or filing our papers in the correct folders together. I needed to let go of control and support my students in becoming independent learners.

The benefits to teaching and learning online are great. First, I believe I provided my students with more instruction online as we didn't lose time to transitions as we do in the classroom, instruction time is less prone to disruptions of different adults walking in the room to get students, and students are able to do what they need to learn. For instance, if a student needs to bounce a ball against the wall to help concentrate online they can do that without disrupting other students. Additionally, you see some kids come out of their shell online because the structure and the tools provide safeguards to participate more fully. Often friends and brick-and-mortar teachers will be skeptical of quality elementary online learning, and although it brought its many challenges, I came to discover many positives along the way. I have become a strong advocate of online education for the right student, as someone who has experienced both environments.

As a teacher I became more flexible than I ever thought I could be. I learned how to use my time in different ways, I practiced letting go of control, and I became a skillful problem solver. Most importantly, I have grown in my professional confidence to make the best decisions for my students and say no to what is not feasible or worthwhile in the classroom. For those new to online teaching, I encourage you to hang in there and embrace the benefits of the model.

Back to School Professional Development

The NCA instructional leaders, like the staff, were not aware of the deep pedagogical shift and growth experience staff would experience by switching to online teaching when planning the back-to-school professional development workshops. The focus of these sessions was equipping staff with the tools and knowledge to get started as well as participating in district-wide training that was required for all elementary teachers. The week before school began consisted of live workshops intermixed with work time and team meetings.

In the "online teaching practices" workshop, teachers were introduced to three practical online learning research frameworks written from a secondary (6–12 grade) or higher education context. Overviews of the following frameworks were presented to staff: emotional presence and the Community of Inquiry model

TABLE 5.1 Back to School PD Schedule for NCA Teachers, Fall 2020. Asterisks Indicate District-Wide Training

Topic	Purpose	Time Frame
Welcome Back Support Circles	• Introducing any new staff • Breaking staff into small groups to connect and share about summer • Conduct staff support circles to honor where people are at and how they are feeling • Play a game to build community and joy	2.5 hours
Communication with Multilingual Families*	• Accessing and using district-wide supports for multilingual communication	1.5 hours
Asset-Based Learner Profiles*	• Building and utilizing asset-based learner profiles for each of our online learners	1.5 hours
Online Teaching Practices	• Connecting research to practice, making sense of online pedagogy research for our context	1 hour
Consistent Online Practices	• Asynchronous versus synchronous • Ignite, chunk, chew, review • Lesson development templates • Communication practices	1 hour
Technology Support & Set Up	• Seesaw support • Remind/Texting set up and support • Classroom monitor and webcam set up	2 hours

(Cleveland-Innes & Campbell, 2012), instructional practices of K-12 teachers (DiPietro, 2010) and parent engagement in online learning (Borup et al., 2014). In between each framework, staff engaged in discussion-based, small group activities in breakout rooms with virtual whiteboards. Within the activities the staff co-constructed ideas for how the practices and findings from the frameworks may apply to the elementary online context and reflected on how their instructional practices might need to change or adjust for their new role. The activities modeled the ignite, chunk, chew, and review instructional strategy, the use of breakout rooms—including giving specific roles—and using different collaborative technology platforms to share ideas. Themes from teacher reflections include the importance of relationships and community, the importance of teacher presence through personality and facilitation, and the need for open-ended and student-centered assessments. These pre-reflections were a brief introduction to the learning and growth teachers would experience in their new online role.

Instructional Coaching

Once the school year launched, professional development consisted of a variety of just-in-time workshops, coaching and problem solving with school and district leadership, and cross-pollinating ideas with colleagues. The lead team of cross departmental district leaders supported the grade level groups as instructional coaches throughout the year through weekly meetings to discuss challenges and successes that groups and individuals were experiencing. The common questions or issues that arose across the groups would dictate the topics for future staff meetings or professional development. The lead team noticed the staff collectively struggling during October of 2020, and this cry for help from teachers was also noted on staff surveys led by the University of Minnesota partners.

Teachers were overwhelmed with work, having difficulty keeping up, and expressing that work was having a negative impact on their wellbeing. The leadership team planned a meeting in early November to problem solve issues *with* the teachers. Inspired by a motivational video (Corduff, 2019), the staff were asked to identify the stressors they were juggling while teaching at NCA. On a slide within the meeting, there were circles representing the various balls everyone was juggling, and staff were asked to type directly onto the slides to share their list. Common responses were creating all of the multimedia lessons within Seesaw, communicating with families, the multitude of meetings, providing feedback on student work, gathering materials, and differentiating.

After the responses were shared the group collectively categorized what they had typed in the circles as either a glass or rubber ball. The glass balls were essential to the program and integral to the success of the school day; while the rubber balls were things that could be dropped if needed and "wouldn't be the end of the world." Each categorized stressor was given its own slide with the title "Solutions for Problem Solving."

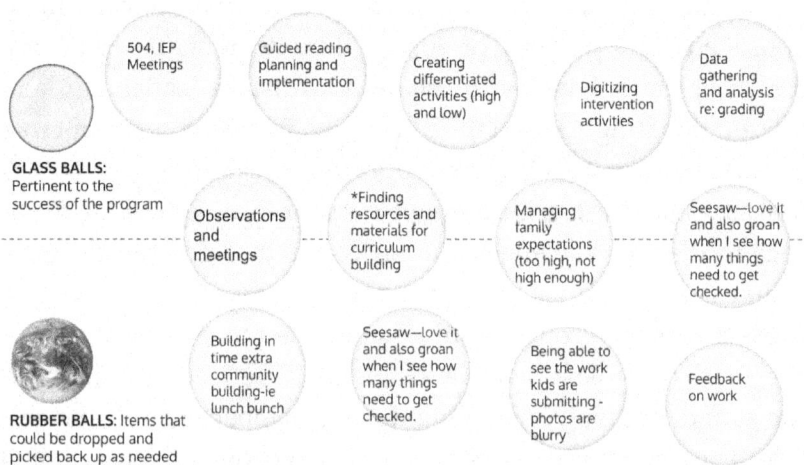

FIGURE 5.1 Slide from October glass and rubber ball problem-solving session

For the rubber balls, the prompt asked, "This ball can drop when needed for teachers and staff. What potential solutions or norms can we create to allow this ball to drop when people need to do so?" For the glass balls, the prompt asked, "Glass balls have to stay, but what are potential solutions for making this glass ball more manageable?" The staff went slide by slide and offered strategies.

The result was a sharing of resources, discussions of philosophy (did teachers need to record all the videos or could they use preexisting videos from reliable sources? did all Seesaw activities need feedback?), a decision to shift professional learning community meetings to a time to distribute responsibilities across teams, and the permission to skip staff meetings and watch the recording. The glass ball conversation revealed that teachers needed more time and a large outcome of the problem solving session was the addition of teacher work days into the monthly schedules after input from the parent advisory committee (see Chapter 9). More importantly, what resulted from the meeting was staff feeling heard and truly supported by leadership. This November "rubber and glass ball" meeting was a common reflection in the spring teacher focus groups as they were not used to leaders hearing their struggles and agreeing to solutions. While it was not your traditional teacher professional development, it was a learning experience and it changed the conversation from what was problematic to designing solutions.

Spotlight on Practice: Doing More by Doing Less, an Exercise in Glass and Rubber Balls

Sara Loftus, New Code Academy, Second Grade Teacher

In October of last year our whole staff was beyond swamped. It felt like we were in the deep end of the pool with weights on. It was constant problem solving, while trying to learn how to teach online and simply survive as a human in a pandemic. We were doing so much thinking about our students and spending an excessive amount of time and energy building lessons that we didn't have the capacity left to figure out how to make the situation better for us as teachers. We were stressed, tired, and feeling like we were not doing anything well, both personally and professionally. Holly met with us as grade-level teams and as a whole staff to hear about our struggles and help us lighten our load. Through the glass and rubber balls activity, we determined things that we as individuals as well as a team were going to let drop if need be. We needed to lighten the load of what we were giving kids and ourselves.

For me, one of the biggest challenges was my commute to and from work. Despite that commute only being going down one flight of stairs to my desk in the basement and back upstairs to go "home," I was having trouble being at the right location at the appropriate time. I would work at my desk each night until 11 pm and then be too stressed to sleep leading to a cycle of being constantly tired in the morning and late to staff meetings. As a group we felt a lot of pressure to give our students the same level of education they would receive in a physical school and were overcompensating and overworking ourselves.

Through our glass and rubber ball discussions a few revelations emerged for me:

1. **Do less:** We were spending too much time making presentation slides beautiful and perfecting instructional videos. We found ways to divide our work as grade-level peers and simplify the experience for us and the students. It was by doing less that we ultimately were able to do more as we were better, rested teachers and students had an appropriate amount of work.
2. **Forgive yourself and others:** Hearing how common some of the glass and rubber balls were made me feel relieved that it wasn't just me not keeping up. Everyone works differently so knowing what other people needed in order to be their best self as well as a collective permission to miss a staff meeting or leave a committee led to a more empathetic team.

3. **Self-care:** I don't mean a pedicure or buying yourself something nice (although those are both great). I mean setting boundaries for what time you will walk away from your desk. Walk away. It will still be there tomorrow; whatever it is you can do it tomorrow.

We didn't know what we didn't know. Luckily, we had a leader who could see we were struggling and actually listened. She made structural changes based on our feedback and gave us true permission and encouragement to scale back our efforts. In my experience, education leaders often give lip service to teachers feeling overwhelmed by adding more to their plate. Holly stayed cognizant and protective of our time and mental health and, in turn, we felt motivated and supported.

Another just-in-time professional development workshop was a teacher-led "unconference" in February of 2021. Modeled after the widely used EdCamp model, the design of the workshop was for-teachers and by-teachers. The staff offered up

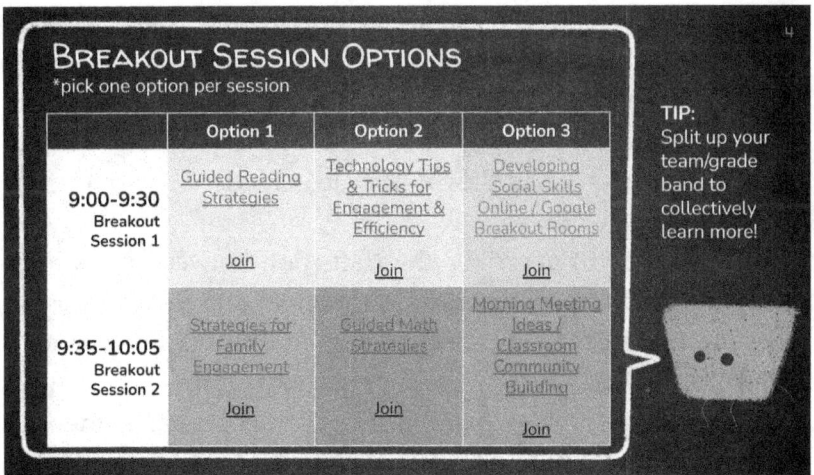

FIGURE 5.2 February schedule for teacher professional development unconference

instructional areas they wanted additional support in, and other staff members who felt confident in their ideas and strategies in that area led informal sharing of processes and resources. The morning was filled with concrete problem solving, cross-pollinating strategies that worked, colleague community building, and teachers having autonomy of their learning. NCA staff knowledge about online pedagogy and teaching strategies had grown substantially. Roles had reversed from the back-to-school workshop week, and the instructional leaders became the workshop learners.

End of the Year Reflective Focus Groups

At the end of the year, professional development focused on reflection and documentation. The teachers had a substantial year of professional growth, most of which was contextually situated within their daily experience as an online teacher. The University of Minnesota research-practice partners led focus groups designed as reflective discussions to give teachers a chance to review their year and document their thoughts. Using the Community of Inquiry model as a prompt, the educators were asked to share specific instructional strategies they had used within the online modality. They were also asked to reflect on professional growth, equity, family engagement, and advice to new online teachers. As it was the end of the year, the teachers seemed relaxed and had the capacity to consider these questions summatively.

DiPietro (2010) describes the transition between brick-and-mortar to online teaching as "**fluid practice**" and the act of using different instructional strategies has an impact on teacher's underlying beliefs about how students learn and what teachers' roles are in that process (p. 336). Fluid practice was evident in teacher focus groups conducted at the end of year one. Staff's reflections on the biggest differences between teaching online and in brick-and-mortar classrooms are not insights that could be easily covered in a workshop, but are learned through experiencing the online modality in practice. In the following section are the NCA teachers conceptualizations of their own fluid practice collected during the end of year focus groups.

Informal Checks of Student Work are Not as Available

Brick-and-mortar teachers regularly walk around the room to see if their students are understanding the information or need more support. This quick check often happens unbeknownst to the students and allows teachers to support individuals, grab a small group of students, extend the activity for those who complete it quickly, or design future lessons. Online, live instruction requires students to point the camera down at their work (with varying degrees of success), and the teacher needs to try to decipher by reading upside down and without the ability to zoom in on the student's work. This resulted in teachers needing to use formative assessment activities differently and more frequently throughout live instruction and utilize a variety of independent learning to capture different ways of knowing (see Chapters 7 & 8 for more examples).

Time Works Differently Within Online Learning

In online learning, not only do teachers plan the live instruction for whole and small groups, as well as independent (and often differentiated) activities, they are building the multimedia and operating within the learning management systems that make the delivery possible. Individual feedback to student work is a bigger component of online pedagogy, and the feedback loop can take longer. First, the student submits the assignment via a learning management system—again NCA prioritizes performance tasks when possible so work is often in a multimedia format—the teacher then needs to review and add written or recorded feedback, and then the student needs to listen or read the feedback and take action. Additionally, the planning and pick up of materials also requires teachers to have their plans developed months in advance and leads to less flexibility to go make a quick copy or purchase something the night before your lesson.

Engagement Must Remain a Priority and Teachers' Sense of Control Needs to Adapt

In a brick-and-mortar school the teacher generally has control over the physical environment. For example, they can turn down the lights, put away items that may distract students, or control the sounds students hear while working independently. In an online environment, teachers have control over what is happening within the class video meeting, such as muting students who have loud background noise or requiring them to raise their hand to participate in the conversation. However, teachers cannot control what is happening in the physical space the students are learning in. Teachers can ask a student, for example, to put away their toys or turn off the television during the meeting, but ultimately cannot reach through the screen. Additionally, teachers do not know what is happening or have control over students' learning environments when they are completing independent activities. It is a more productive strategy to focus on engagement rather than control by making both live and independent learning active and fun to keep students' interest and stay cognizant of their brains' ability to focus between breaks.

A Stronger Home to School Partnership

Elementary learners are not home alone; there is a learning coach who is in the building (oftentimes the same room) as the student. NCA teachers were engaged in consistent and more informal communication with the learning coaches (see Chapter 10). If a student was missing in a meeting, needed comfort, or was having a difficult time following the meeting norms, the teachers and adults would be in contact through messaging or email. Additionally, the walls between classroom and home dissolved which generally led to deeper relationships and empathy for each other. For example, lower-elementary parents and younger siblings often join morning meeting activities, and class communities know each other's family from seeing them in the background of video feeds every day. The intimacy that the modality creates as well as the importance of the learning coach as the adult caring for the child in their physical environment, creates a different relationship between teachers and caregivers.

Teaching Online Requires New Boundaries and Routines

Brick-and-mortar teachers travel to work, connect with colleagues in the hallway, and go home at the end of the day (not that they do not take work with them). NCA teachers primarily work from home and had to create new routines to switch into work mode as well as decompress at the end of the day. Normally this would often happen on the ride home when teaching at a brick-and-mortar school. Related to the section above about home partnerships, there was also an increased amount of communication happening outside of contract hours as a result of the increased relationships, modes of communication, and the walls between school and home being dissolved as well for the students. Teachers tended to navigate these boundaries differently based on what felt right for them.

> **Spotlight on Practice:**
> **Misconceptions About Online Learning**

Tori Nienaltowski, New Code Academy, Fourth Grade Teacher

Coming into NCA, my assumption was that there would not be as much community and relationships as there is in the physical classroom. I just did not think it was possible for kids in their individual houses staring at computers to build relationships with others through a screen. This was the biggest misconception I had about online education, and actually relationships are just as possible online and even more important for my students' learning. We spend time daily building community and relationships both between students and between myself and the students. Through structured get-to-know-you activities in morning meetings to more less structured activities such as playing online board games, partnering students to work together, or having Friday fun time we build community quickly.

Another misconception I had about teaching online was how big the transition to becoming an online learner is. This way of learning and being a student is very different from what they have experienced before. I quickly learned I needed to slow down and be much more specific when we started the year. Every direction needs to be broken down into small, individual steps at first. When I am introducing a new tool I share my screen, I talk through and point out every move, and the students practice navigating the same moves on their screen. Repetition is huge, and I always ensure my students can see the directions, hear the directions, and practice the directions. Even though I feel I am being very specific, the students always have a lot of questions because they want to make sure they are understanding and getting it correct. These questions help me get better at giving instructions. I practice the same advice that I give to my students: take a breath, step back, and remind yourself we are all new here.

The time building relationships and building the digital competencies was worth it as by the end of the first month, students are able to engage in learning and have a whole community of people to call on for help. Rather than slowly going through the specific steps of where to find their assignment, I can just say, "Go to Seesaw and find your math assignment." Their questions for me are about the learning content, not where to find something or navigate the technology. Students also know how and when to reach out to their peers for support if I am not available or if there is a classmate they know can help them. I often will put students into a breakout room together to troubleshoot technology or peer tutor an assignment. Elementary students are capable of being independent online learners. We as adults need to provide them time and scaffolds to build the skills and relationships that will make the academic year successful.

Curriculum and Lesson Documentation

As most teachers were building the plane while they flew it, instructional leaders wanted to ensure that curriculum documents, activities, and slideshows were in a place that others could access in the future. This documentation took place through "curriculum checklist" meetings led by the digital learning coordinator with each grade level and through using an interdisciplinary checklist for teachers to talk through each unit, identify what revisions were needed and show where the materials were housed. There were curriculum dollars to support summer 2021 curriculum work if teachers were interested. It was a moment to review notes or ideas of how lessons or activities could be revised or improved to ensure these next steps were documented.

Based on the experience from year one and the teacher reflective focus groups, the following practices are recommended for instructional leaders in supporting their teachers' fluid practice:

1. **Support the evolution from brick-and-mortar to online teaching process.** The most seasoned teachers who could be described as highly flexible and having a growth mindset will be challenged in new ways. There is no workshop that can magically turn someone into an online teacher. This is an important idea to remember for year two and beyond when a school might have a mix of experienced and new online teachers. The new online teachers still need space for this evolution to take place.
2. **Provide as much time as possible.** Do not fill every minute of staff meetings or scheduled PD. This evolution involves a lot of trial and error, searching for resources, and connecting with colleagues. Remember that learning happens through doing, failing, succeeding, reflecting, and revising, and all of those actions take time.
3. **Divide and coach to provide just-in-time support and problem solving.** Ensure that every team has an

instructional leader who will be present as a team *member*, not a boss. Listen to the current problems of practice and follow up with actions that actually support (finding resources, developing sustainable solutions). Ensure that the instructional leaders who are present in these team spaces are connecting regularly to identify what teachers need versus something that might require structural change or whole-staff growth.

4. **Expect to change program design elements based on teacher feedback.** Leading an online school is a new endeavor for most instructional leaders. The original program design or approach will likely need iterations, and educators should have voice in that change. It is a great opportunity to model a flexible mindset and be a responsive educator who does what is best for students.

5. **Prioritize the power of collegial presence.** Research or "experts" are often sought to solve problems when the answers are already present. If given the opportunity through time and autonomy, teachers are talented problem solvers and team members. Sometimes, the issue is that everyone is trying to solve the same problem or not maximizing capacity by dividing and conquering. Building a community amongst staff will pay dividends when educators feel they trust and are supported by colleagues.

It was a year of growth and change for the teachers and the instructional leaders. The leadership approaches that seemed most successful mimicked what is recommended for teachers: build community, seek feedback, try new approaches, and be okay with changing the model.

Questions to Consider When Developing a Professional Development Plan:
- What training and skills do teachers need in order to use the hardware and software for teaching online?

- How can you be both planful in growing educators but flexible to their "just-in-time" needs?
- What are the consistent practices you want all online teachers to follow?
- What professional support, in addition to trainings, can be provided to teachers for their shift into online teaching?
- What are responsibilities or meetings that can be offloaded or paused to create time and attention for teachers?

References

Borup, J., West, R. E., Graham, C. R., & Davies, R. S. (2014). The adolescent community of engagement framework: A lens for research on K-12 online learning. *Journal of Technology and Teacher Education*, *22*(1), 107–129.

Cleveland-Innes, M., & Campbell, P. (2012). Emotional presence, learning, and the online learning environment. *The International Review of Research in Open and Distributed Learning*, *13*(4), 269–292.

Corduff, L. (2019). *The juggle is real!* https://lisacorduff.com/juggling-video/

Dipietro, M. (2010). Virtual school pedagogy: The instructional practices of K-12 virtual school teachers. *Journal of Educational Computing Research*, *42*(3), 327–354.

6

Launching the First 20 Days Online

This chapter will detail the first 20 days of New Code Academy that seeks to build students' digital competencies, grow classroom community, and establish norms and routines for online learning. This intentional planning and prioritization before jumping into academics makes the rest of the school year efficient and accessible.

In elementary schools, the first few weeks of a new year are a time to reintroduce students to an academic environment including establishing norms and routines, and building a classroom community. Those approaches are also true for online learning; however, the academic environment is virtual and necessitates that students have digital competencies to engage. The development of classroom communities needs to be hyper intentional to facilitate peer learning activities—students may be unfamiliar with being social through technology— and to create an inclusive and welcoming learning environment. Additionally, the norms and routines of online schooling require more independent learning skills to navigate the schedule, complete asynchronous work, and self-regulate without the constant engagement of an adult learning coach.

Planning the First 20 Days

To begin planning for the first 20 days of school, the summer curriculum development team spent time unpacking what students at each grade level would need to know or be able to do related to using the technology tools for online learning and navigating the rituals and routines of the day (see brainstorm table below). It was the belief of NCA instructional leaders that taking the time to build independent learners would make the rest of the year go smoother and faster. Additionally, ensuring that *all students* have the knowledge and skills to participate in online learning provides a more equitable learning environment. The first month would not introduce formal academic units and would remain sacred to building students' online learning capacity and engagement (Gonzalez & Kitchen, 2020).

To support educators in moving from the abstract brainstorm of the first 20 days to concrete outcomes for the first

Teacher Digital Competency Brainstorm Ideas for the First 20 Days.

Use of **Seesaw** by teacher and students	**Safety online**, purposeful use of time	How to easily **share results** (videos, pics, etc)	Connecting **parents** before school starts
Any **other online platforms** students will use, i.e. raz-kids, freckle etc. . .	**Tech tips** to train students with Seesaw and other tools you want to use	Seesaw; **submitting**, reviewing work that might have been returned or has **feedback**, blog, announcements	**Ethical** use of online resources. Respect ideas of other students, even though they're not face-to-face
Password cards/ show them systems to keep track of login information	Seesaw **training for parents** Connect families to **family app**	Checking for **feedback**, realistic feedback expectations	Go **slow**. Post all passwords in an accessible place
Google Workspace of Tools and Seesaw **features**	Internet **accessibility** and troubleshooting any issues that come up	Step-by-step instructions with **visual aids** and audio recordings	**Explanation** videos and practice activities

TABLE 6.1 Excerpt From First 20 Days Planning Template

Weekly High-Level Planning
Tech competencies, community/relationship building, and rituals/routines are the three areas of focus for the first 20 days. Your team will brainstorm everything you think needs to be included in these areas and then sequence/prioritize them by placing them into the template for week 1, 2, 3, and 4. Use the questions and prompts below to brainstorm.

Tech Competencies	Community and Relationship Building	Rituals & Routines
What tools do we need to know how to use? • Seesaw • Google Meet • Flipgrid • Padlet • Google Tools What skills do we need to be able to use those tools? • Muting microphone • Checking Seesaw activities • Accessing daily work • Joining a Google Meet, etc.	Who is in our class? How are we connected? How will we get to know one another? How will we build connections and relationships online? Where can we provide opportunities for families to get involved? How can we utilize the first 20 days to humanize our children? • How can we address what children have been through this summer? • How can we address the pandemic and its impact?	What does our day look like? What expectations are there for teacher and student? What classroom rituals and routines might transfer F2F to online? Where can we build opportunities for students to give feedback? What are our block routines? What are our morning meeting routines? What are our end-of-day routines? What are our academic routines (e.g. first 20 days of math, ELA, etc.)? What are our culminating assessment routines?

20 days, instructional leaders developed a scope and sequence template by week, day, and block of time (see table 6.1 above). The template included prompts and questions grounded in the instructional framework (see Chapter 1) including brain breaks, multi-modal instruction, language supports, and culturally responsive teaching. As a companion resource to the template, teachers were provided a tool with guidance related to content and order of the lesson plans. From a leadership perspective, it

also defined concrete expectations of what the school day should look like and served as a tool to communicate to parents what they should expect from the first 20 days. Excerpts from the template are included in this chapter, and the full template can be found in the appendix.

Digital Competencies

Technologically, all students need to know how to use every official school learning platform and its tools and features, as well as the hardware of their school-provided Chromebook. Teachers identified these competencies by documenting every step from turning on the device, signing into a website with a name and password, to submitting an assignment within Seesaw. Digital competencies include effective troubleshooting and persevering through technical issues—which are common in online learning. Teachers can model staying calm and verbally talking through tech problems as well as showing compassion and support to students who are experiencing glitches. In addition to knowing how to use the technological tools, students should develop skills in using the learning platforms to engage in content and show what they know. Every step to access, use, and troubleshoot these tools needs to be explicitly taught, retaught, and practiced.

Routines and Rituals

Routines and rituals that support online learning begin from the moment the student wakes up to when they sleep, as students generally live and learn in the same space. This includes setting up their learning space with their school materials and putting away items that may cause distractions. Ideally the students should know their schedule and join live class meetings at the correct time with supports from learning coaches at the younger grades. Supports for schedule routines include timers, alarm clocks, notifications, and paper calendars. Each class intentionally practices and discusses the daily schedule, the ways to participate in live meetings, strategies for working independently, and using the lunch break to go screen-free and get physically active.

Community Building

NCA staff and leaders believe that developing relationships between students and with teachers is crucial. Having no personal connection to the class community makes students more apt to skipping lessons. The goal in the first 20 days is to establish a community and welcoming class environment that students want to come back to everyday. This includes everyone knowing each other's names and general interests through opportunities to hear from and talk to their classmates. Through games and activities, students should feel comfortable and confident in socializing and learning with peers in live class meet-ups. Additionally, this learning partnership between the student and the teacher should include the learning coach with all three parties feeling comfortable communicating with each other if there are ever questions or needs.

Spotlight on Practice: Breaking Down Large Digital Learning Goals into Scaffolded Lessons

Allie Kalkman, New Code Academy, Kindergarten Teacher

When I mention that I teach kindergarten in an online setting, I'm met with wide eyes and disbelief. What about play time? How can they be independent? How do students make friends? Do they need an adult near them all day? The answer to these questions is careful planning, scaffolding, and appropriate time for learning and developing these skills.

Our task at the beginning of the year is to quickly teach students a wide array of technology skills without letting them become dependent on the adults in their home. We start by creating a large list of skills that students need to complete their daily work. These skills fall into three categories: Google Meet, Seesaw, and physical items. We prioritize skills based on the difficulty level, necessity, and congruence with academic outcomes and physical materials. We then create a tool introduction calendar to see how skills overlap, align, and build upon one another. The calendar helps us plan our lessons and is shared with other staff working with our students (Figure 6.1).

Kindergarten Tool Introduction

Physical Tool
Digital Tool

Monday	Tuesday	Wednesday	Thursday	Friday
Pre-teaching to families: -Log into tablet -Log into Google Meet -Log into Seesaw			-Crayon -Join/Leave Meet -Mute/Unmute -Find activities/lightbulb -Multipage Activities -Add response/green check -Pen and (preview) eraser	-Pencil -Pen (size/color) -Eraser -Move tool -Review Seesaw and Meet
-Glue Stick -Play Doh -Camera (Seesaw) -Review Seesaw/Meet	Listen to feedback from teacher	-Tweezers/Poms -Draft mode	-Dry Erase Marker/Eraser -Camera on/off in Google Meet	-Scissors -Fine Motor Bags
-Voice Recording -Breakout Room with Adults	Arrow with voice recording	Name Puzzles		
Switching Classes in Seesaw		Blog		

FIGURE 6.1 Kindergarten Tool Introduction Calendar

Day 1

Our primary goal on day one is to make students feel successful and excited to come back for day two. The first day requires nine technology skills just to be present for school: log into device, log into Seesaw, find activities, click meeting link, join meeting, make sure camera is on, unmute to ask questions, mute when finished, and hang up. We send families information on this process prior to the first day of school and offer technology support during Meet the Teacher conferences. On day one, we ultimately teach students three Google Meet skills (mute, unmute, and hang up) in addition to leading a guided discovery with crayons.

Week 1

Week one goals include grasping physical tools to show our learning, practicing pre-writing skills, getting to know our classmates, and practicing digital skills. We teach students how to use crayons and pencils and show them how to access their written work for the first several weeks of school. We practice Google Meet a lot and give students multiple chances to unmute and mute each day. We introduce Seesaw learning tools by teaching the pen tool and having students trace pre-written lines just as we had done on paper. Next, we teach students how to vary the color and size of the pen to create and color. Finally, we teach the move tool to practice simple sorting.

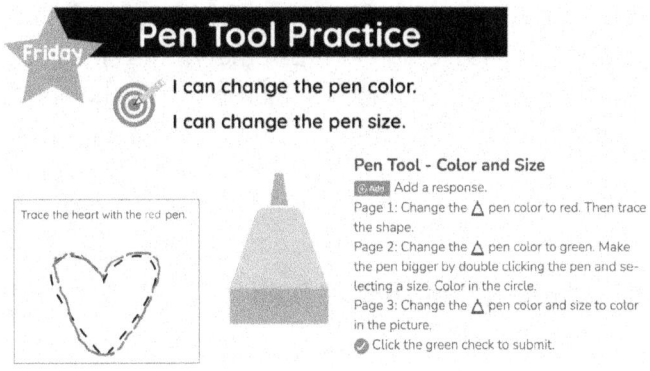

FIGURE 6.3 Kindergarten Seesaw activity: Teaching pen color and size

Week 2

The second week of school brings a new routine by learning alphabet and number activities. Each day we focus on a different letter and number and slowly add pages to our Seesaw activities that practice new tools. We teach students how to take photos of their work since a majority of work is done on paper. We introduce how to watch instructional videos, listen to directions via voice notes, and listen to teacher comments with their families. These skills allow students to complete activities without adults needing to be close by to read or explain directions.

Beyond

Throughout the remainder of the month, we introduce the microphone and arrow to practice letter and number recognition. We slowly increase the complexity of activities and allow students to practice previous tools in different ways. Over time, we encourage families to give students more ownership of previous adult responsibilities such as finding meeting links, joining meets, and navigating Seesaw. We use fall conferences as an opportunity to check in with families about which skills students still need support with.

Parent feedback regarding independent learning and technology skills has been positive. Many note they are surprised with how independent their learners are during class time. With scaffolding, routine, and repetitive practice, our students flourish with technology and are able to access and complete a wide variety of learning activities.

Lessons Learned in the First 20 Days

Emotions were high with anticipation and uncertainty amongst the staff on the first day of school and the piloting of the first 20 days unit. Teachers shared that the first few weeks came with many awkward moments of silence or technology issues that derailed the plans but was generally a success. The top reflection was how slow and simple the instruction needed to be, which was much more granular and explicit than teachers had planned. Consistency and practice with the tools and procedures became key as teachers were finding ways to introduce the technological tools in activities that also built class community. As the class relationships strengthened and comfort in the modality grew, the class flowed more naturally, and there were less awkward moments. "It will get better" is a common refrain from the NCA teachers about the first 20 days.

NCA teachers who are in their second year recommend simplifying the first 20 days by removing any unnecessary barriers. For example, the lower elementary classes begin the first 20 days spending most of their day in a live meeting (30 minutes on, 30 minutes off) so that students can first learn the technology before introducing how to use a schedule or independent learning work. They also recommend letting go of the pressure of diving into academic content as this period of establishing culture and equipping students with the skills they need to engage in the learning is essential for the rest of the year to succeed.

Spotlight on Practice: Leading "Meet the Teacher" Conferences to Build Trust and Relationships

Emilee Vlasin, New Code Academy, Third Grade Teacher

Similar to brick-and-mortar teaching, online teaching is all about relationships. The week before school begins, we set up virtual meetings with each family and student to get to know each other and discuss the student's unique assets. This meeting sets up lines of communication, provides opportunities to establish expectations, and gives me a quick glance into each student's life as well as possible support they may need. I begin this meeting by showing pictures of my interests, my family, and a silly picture of myself in third grade. Once I have put my personality out there, it seems to break the ice and create an environment where people are willing to share. I then go through the following list of questions to learn more about the student and build their asset-based profile:

- To Student: Tell me about yourself! What do you like to do at home? What else do you like?
- To Family: Tell me about your student! What are important things that I should know?
- Who does your child live with? Do they have another home they live in? Who lives in that home? (Where does your child spend time?)
- What holidays and traditions are important to your family? How do you celebrate them? What is the student's favorite? Why?
- What are your child's strengths?
- What areas or skills would you like to see your child grow in this year (academically, socially, or otherwise)?
- Who will be supporting your child during the school day? Who is the best person to contact?
- We value seeing our students during the day as they are learning, so we ask that students keep their videos/cameras on during our meetings. Is there any reason your child would need to have their camera off?
- What will your child's workspace look like? (Is there a space that is distraction free, away from TV, siblings, etc.?) (Will your child need more than one set of supplies?)
- To Student: What would you like to learn about this year? What do you feel like you are good at in school? What is frustrating or challenging for you at school?
- Is there anything else you would like me to know about your child or family?

As the student shares, I try to make a personal connection to one of their likes or interests. One time I scored bonus points with a student when he found out that I also have a dirt bike! This meeting also creates space for families to be vulnerable and share about things that might be impacting their child. For instance, one family shared with me that they had recently experienced a big loss, and we discussed how I could support their child socially and emotionally throughout the year.

Within the conference we discuss if there are any reasons the camera might be off during the day, material pick up, and we create space for the student and families to ask me any questions they might have. I close the meeting with a game of "this or that" in which I use slides with two choices for students to pick from. Some of the slides are just fun questions like the ability to fly or be invisible and others ask students to choose between math or reading. The relationships built in these conferences set the groundwork for trust and communication between the families, students, and myself.

Families and the First 20 Days

When time is spent building routines and rituals within the brick-and-mortar classroom, most of that work is not seen by families. A few parents reached out during the first week of school because they were not seeing math or a standard reading lesson and grew concerned. Communication was sent out after the first week to families reiterating the prioritization of building community, rituals and routines, and digital competencies. Ultimately, the skills their children would gain in the first 20 days would allow the adult learning coaches to take a step back and not feel they were in a pseudo-home schooling situation. Even for students that have historically experienced more difficulty building independent learning skills, feedback from families shows they are surprised at what their child is able to do without their help. Hearing, "Wow, I didn't see my second grader all day" is a celebratory moment for the program as a sign that independent learning skills are developing.

The beginning of the school year is also an opportunity for school leadership to make calls and emails to families. It is a busy time of year but the connections made with follow-up communication are important. Choosing online school is a big transition for many families who have likely heard stereotypes that online learning is "less-than" or took a leap of faith to find a school setting that was right for their child(ren). The calls focus on how they feel the launch of the school year went, celebrate successes, answer questions, solve any issues they are experiencing, and collect feedback. Calls to families are not unique to the online school but without the physical location and "main office" families are familiar with, these calls remind families they have school resources and contacts beyond the classroom teacher (see Chapter 9 for more information).

Spotlight on Practice: Creating Access Points for All Students to Thrive Online

Ruth Murray, NCA Lead Team & Special Education Instructional Strategies & Digital Learning Manager, Bloomington Public Schools

Some might say not everyone is capable of learning online or that students aren't developing the social skills they need for the real world, but I see it differently. New Code Academy is changing the environment and education variables and allowing the academics to move front and center while building community and social skills in new and unique ways that better fit individual student needs.

Many of our special education students and families have found success at NCA. We have kids who really struggle with some social pieces but are very academically capable. With face-to-face social components removed, those students can now focus on their strengths. For example, we have a student who was placed in a setting three classroom in their brick-and-mortar school and has now been discontinued from special education services at NCA. The behaviors we saw in the building are not taking place online, and academics are accelerating. Other students have dealt with bullying in the brick-and-mortar setting and their parents are now breathing a sigh of relief, because their child is laughing, participating and feels like a part of school for the first time.

A key framework for creating an environment where all students can find success is Universal Design for Learning (UDL). The online format has prompted teachers to think deeper about how to best meet students' needs by first considering the <u>why</u>. What is the why behind your lesson? Why are students learning this? What do you want them to know and do? When the <u>why</u> is established, teachers can build access points based on different student needs and design to the edges. Access points could include providing a student with the audio version while their peers read or sentence stems to support student participation in group book discussions. One place UDL practices are crucial is the first 20 days of school unit where the <u>why</u> is building independent learners that can participate in school online. We've found that there is a difference between *building* independent learners and *expecting* them to be independent learners.

Many students and their families, especially those that might receive multiple services, struggle with how to access and implement the schedule. One strategy we started this year was a visual, concise schedule with links out to the different meetings students would attend throughout the day. We can't make assumptions about what students know coming into an online learning setting. As NCA staff continue to learn and document what we expect a student to know and do by the end of the first 20 days, we can use more UDL strategies such as building an age-appropriate rubric that lays out the different levels and entry points to teach skills. Some students will come in at a higher level of digital competence, ready to open up a Google document when directed. Other students will need scaffolds such as written steps or a visual to remind them "how" to access the google doc or create a new one.

There is no one-size-fits-all for education, and there is an opportunity cost everywhere. Our families who were looking for an online experience, not just for health reasons, but are seeking a better fit for their children are really happy. It makes me feel super proud to be a part of the New Code Academy online community.

The first 20 days drive the culture and student experience within the classroom and school for the rest of the year. Regrounding in an academic environment after a summer break and becoming an online learner both benefit from practicing norms and building community. While the NCA teachers have designed and iterated their first 20 days plan, more needs to be investigated and defined related to age-appropriate independent learning skills for elementary online learners. This includes building executive functioning and self-regulation skills and creating brain-based access points. Parents and teachers are often amazed when they see how comfortable and confident a K-5 learner can become in online school.

Question to Consider When Supporting Students in Becoming Online Learners:
- What are all the skills and knowledge that students need to be successful digitally within the program both with devices and applications?
- How can you teach students digital competencies and routines through community building?
- What does it mean to be an independent learner?
- Based on the students' ages, what additional scaffolds or alterations to the first 20 days would set them up for success in the rest of the school year?

Reference

Gonzalez, J., & Kitchen, M. (2020, July 5). *9 ways online teaching should be different than face-to-face.* Cult of Pedagogy. https://www.cultofpedagogy.com/9-ways-online-teaching/

7

Leading Live Instruction

Live or synchronous instruction is a core program design feature of New Code Academy that affords community learning and effective instruction for K-5 learners. This chapter will share specific strategies, reflections, and guidance on leading live instruction with elementary learners online.

Notably, there are a lot of whole-group and small group instructional practices within the brick-and-mortar classroom that are not effective. Direct instruction is often too long, covers too much information, and forgets to give students enough opportunities to process the content. Ineffective instruction can result in students getting fidgety or chatty because their brains have disengaged and can lead to disciplinary action because the teacher sees the student as off task rather than reflecting on *why* the student is off task. Becoming online educators forced NCA staff to examine whole group and small group instructional time as there is less live instruction so the time together needed to be high quality.

> **Spotlight on Practice: Developmental Needs for Primary Learners**

Kristen Fett, New Code Academy, Kindergarten Teacher

When I first began teaching online, I felt a little out of sorts knowing that families were able to watch me teach in a way they'd never been able to before, unless they'd volunteered in my classroom. I stuck strictly to my lesson plans and left little room for my true, authentic personality to shine through. However, it didn't take long for me to realize that this approach wasn't sustainable—for me or my students. My kindergarteners needed to connect with me more than ever before, and they needed my personality to shine through.

Creating meaningful and lasting relationships with children and families has always been my number one priority as a teacher. Children will not learn unless they develop personal connections with their teachers. For me, that meant being silly, singing songs, reading stories in funny voices, telling stories about my life, and sharing things that are important to me. Although easy in the traditional classroom, it was harder to put it all online where others were listening and watching.

However, once I let my walls down I saw how engaged my online learners were when I shared about my life. I began to feel the same connections develop across a screen that developed so easily in person. Adding personal touches to my online lessons like pictures of my pets, or things I knew my kindergarteners had connections to (hockey, dance, rainbows, animals), helped build their excitement and engagement with the digital activities we were working on. These little things yielded a big impact with my students.

I also quickly realized how important it was to not always rely on Google slideshows, pre-recorded videos, and ready-made resources. Yes, they were amazing tools I could use to add meaning, depth, and excitement to my digital lessons, but they couldn't replace me. My students also needed to hear my voice and watch me teach just as they would if we were together in a traditional classroom setting. For instance, allowing my students to see me holding a book in my hands, turning the pages, listening to me read with expression, and watching me react to every part of the story was a powerful alternative to watching the same book read by someone on YouTube. Rather than play a GoNoodle video for them to watch, I'd also do energizers and brain breaks with my students by modeling and practicing.

Because we did them so often, energizers and brain breaks were especially fun ways to connect with my students. Developmentally, I knew how important it was to include as much movement as possible, both embedded into my lesson but also done authentically when I could see wiggles and distracted students on my screen. In a traditional classroom, breaks happen naturally as students move around the room during transitions between lessons or learning centers. Breaks had to be much more purposeful online, especially if I wanted them to be rooted in academics. Including learning songs about phonics and numbers, body movements like jumping jacks for counting, and directing kids to have a standing conversation in a breakout room were all ways I kept my online learners engaged with movement.

Modeling and practicing these skills together with me was the key in helping my online learners experience success. Teaching my students and modeling how they could tilt their screens up or down helped ensure they were in the center of their screen. Using pictures, visual cues, and simple verbal directions also helped my students be successful with the myriad of activities we were doing together.

Live or synchronous class meetings are the closest online element to brick-and-mortar instruction; however, they require different norms, facilitation, and skills for both students and teachers. Leading instruction through video meetings can feel clunky, quiet, or chaotic at first, but through practicing the modality and building relationships a natural flow begins to develop. Classroom management looks different in that teachers have a full panel of controls that students do not have access to that can mute or remove students or turn on and off features for the class. The skills, routines, and relationships learned in the first 20 days establish the norms for live meetings, but naturally there will be moments when young learners need to be reminded and guided. Live instruction is most successful when it is active, participatory, multimodal, personal, and differentiated.

Active

Within all live lessons, students should be using learning materials such as Play-Doh, paper, pencil, or whiteboards. For a kindergartener at the beginning of the year, this might include making the letters out of Play-Doh with the support of a paper that outlines the letters, and at the end of the year it could look like a nonfiction text packet comparing butterflies and moths with a provided Venn Diagram. Document cameras are a key tool for teachers to model the use of materials within live lesson activities, and students can adjust their camera to point at their desk so the teacher can offer support and identify when it is okay to move on. From a planning perspective, the live lessons need to be mapped out in advance so that students can have any material, copies, mind maps, or workbooks they need sent to them prior (see more info in Chapter 4).

In addition to the kinesthetics offered by using materials, the live lessons should provide students opportunities to communicate learning *through* their bodies. A major way this is supported at NCA is by teaching sign language or other actions that are used during discussions and activities. For instance, in a science lesson on plants, students were taught different hand symbols for stem, leaf, root, flower, and fruit. As pictures of plant specimens were shared, students guessed which part of the plant they were seeing with their bodies before the answer was revealed through class discussion. The actions were used to help the students remember the new concepts and stay engaged.

Students also practice concepts *with* their bodies such as counting by 10s using jumping jacks or going on a scavenger hunt for something in their house that connects with the learning objective or concept from a book.

Participatory

Live lessons should include opportunities for students to contribute, reflect, and problem solve. In addition to staying engaged, students need frequent opportunities for "dialogic talk" which includes students organizing and sharing their thinking out loud as well as hearing others' responses and additions to their ideas (Hammond, 2015, p. 134). In whole-group meetings students raise their hands and participate, but that generally limits how many students can share. Using breakout rooms can maximize opportunities for dialogic talk between students. NCA students are always asking for breakout rooms as there are less people, students can talk more and remain unmuted, and the conversation is less structured. Breakout rooms are introduced to students by practicing low stakes social conversations and are scaffolded with sentence stems. After comfort is built with using breakout rooms, they are used frequently within lessons for small group discussions and activities.

Connecting with an idea: It is sometimes easier to share a new idea than to connect to someone else's idea, here are some ways to help your student connect with what someone else is sharing.

- When you said _____, it reminded me of _____.
- I would feel _____, if _____ happened to me.
- [paraphrase what you heard], that sounds _____.
- Can you tell me more about _____.

FIGURE 7.1 Excerpt from a sentence starter guide created by the parent advisory board to coach students

Spotlight on Practice: Breaking Out of Whole Group Meetings into Smaller Discussions

Sara Loftus, New Code Academy, Second Grade Teacher

Breakout rooms are the equivalent of students spreading out around the classroom and working in groups except that online you cannot see students at all times and families can hear their discussions, both of which can be nerve-racking for teachers. To prepare students to use breakout rooms we discuss what it means to be a good digital citizen as well as what it looks like and sounds like to be respectful and kind. Every morning we review a slide of meeting "Yesses" and meeting "No thank yous." For instance, "Please make sure you have clothes on the top half and the bottom half of your body. If you don't, now is the time to turn off your camera, get dressed, and come back to turn your camera on so we know you are still here. If you have another device out, it should be powered off and put away."

Example of meeting yesses:

- Wear appropriate clothes
- Listen to the speaker
- Find a quiet place
- Raise your hand
- Try your best

Examples of meeting nos:

- No toys and pets (they can be around just no show and tell)
- No television on
- No food or drinks (for the safety of their laptop)

The most common issue that we experience in breakout rooms are students getting off task—as they want to talk about video games, LOL dolls, or let their classmates know that Santa is not real. Seldomly, a family member will notice students are off topic in a breakout room and become concerned. I try to communicate that this also happens in brick-and-mortar classrooms and is not unique to online school. Getting off-topic is a natural occurrence for adults and particularly second graders, but every breakout room activity is an opportunity to practice talking about class content.

We first teach students how to engage in breakout rooms within social, not academic settings. The first month of breakout rooms, we give them a sentence stem that we review all together such as "My favorite thing about fall is . . ." then send them into breakout rooms with a few peers for 2 minutes and then bring them back. We slowly elongate the time and give less structure as students become more comfortable. We host "Talking Tuesdays" during morning meetings to give students extended periods of time to chat about things they are interested in. I will visit different breakout rooms to check in on the conversation, and if any student is having an issue or the people in their room are off task, they can always come back to the main room to get me.

As students show confidence and commitment to our meeting norms, we start using breakout rooms for academic discussions and support. In addition to having "turn and talk" brief conversation in a lesson, during "Working Wednesdays" we put students into breakout rooms based on what they need to get caught up with. This allows them to work collaboratively with others who were focused on the same assignment or just work quietly in a room with a peer. If kids are all caught up, I would ask who they wanted to hang out with and send them into a room together.

Using breakout rooms gives more students opportunities to talk and share. It's where kids are truly building relationships with each other. We could take 5 minutes to hear three students' star (highlights) and wish (opportunity for tomorrow), or we can send them into a breakout room and everyone gets a chance to reflect out loud. Teaching breakout rooms involves a lot of scaffolding and reminders of expectations, but impact on social and academic learning is worth it.

Multimodal

Within the live lessons students experience content and information through a variety of representations including hearing, seeing, and doing. Teachers may develop slides, use an interactive virtual whiteboard, their document camera, or even a physical whiteboard or poster in their video shot. When possible, NCA teachers pair the lesson and activity with videos or media that brings the content to life and provides a connection to the outside world. For instance during Asian American and Pacific Islander Heritage month, first-grade students learned about Maya Lin, the architect and designer of the Vietnam Veterans Memorial. Together they read "Maya Lin: Artist-Architect of Light and Lines" by Jeanne Walker Harvey with beautiful imagery from Dow Phumiruk. After reading the book together, the teacher shared the Vietnam Veterans Memorial Fund website (vvmf.org) on her screen, and the class took a virtual tour of the memorial designed by Maya Lin.

Personal

Students are more engaged when the teacher is personable and adds their unique flair to reading books, leading movement activities, and recording their own videos rather than pressing play on a video found on the internet. Teachers command attention when they are excited, passionate, and energetic on the screen, have a light to illuminate their face on the video, and a purposefully designed room behind them to showcase their personality. For example, a kindergarten teacher led a lesson on sequencing using a bowl of cereal and her document camera. She led the students through some silly antics as she did things in the wrong order, making a mess visible to the students. She created connection moments when students were able to share their favorite breakfast food as she was preparing hers. Instead

FIGURE 7.2 Kindergarten teacher's home workspace and camera background 2021

of teaching a skill with a sequencing worksheet, students experienced the lesson through a memorable activity with their teacher.

Differentiated

The NCA program collects formative data within whole group meetings, breakout rooms, small group learning, and 1:1 student-teacher check-ins to adapt and design instruction, interventions, and groupings. Formative assessments happen frequently within live instruction using the district's Gradual Release of Responsibility Framework (GRR) that helps teachers determine appropriate instructional scaffolds to support students towards performing skills or knowledge independently (Fisher & Frey, 2013). The GRR framework can also align with Hammond's (2015) "ignite, chunk, chew, and review" instructional approach to design culturally responsive instruction and collect formative assessment information in parallel. For example, a kindergarten math learning target is "I can use a ten frame to make the number 10." As a whole group the teacher begins with the students using their whole body to chant count to ten while performing an action (ignite). Next the teacher introduces the concept through a brief direct instruction using Google Slides or the document camera as a visual (chunk).

After, the students participate in guided instruction. The teacher introduces and models a tens frame template and counters for the activity as the students manipulate and mimic the

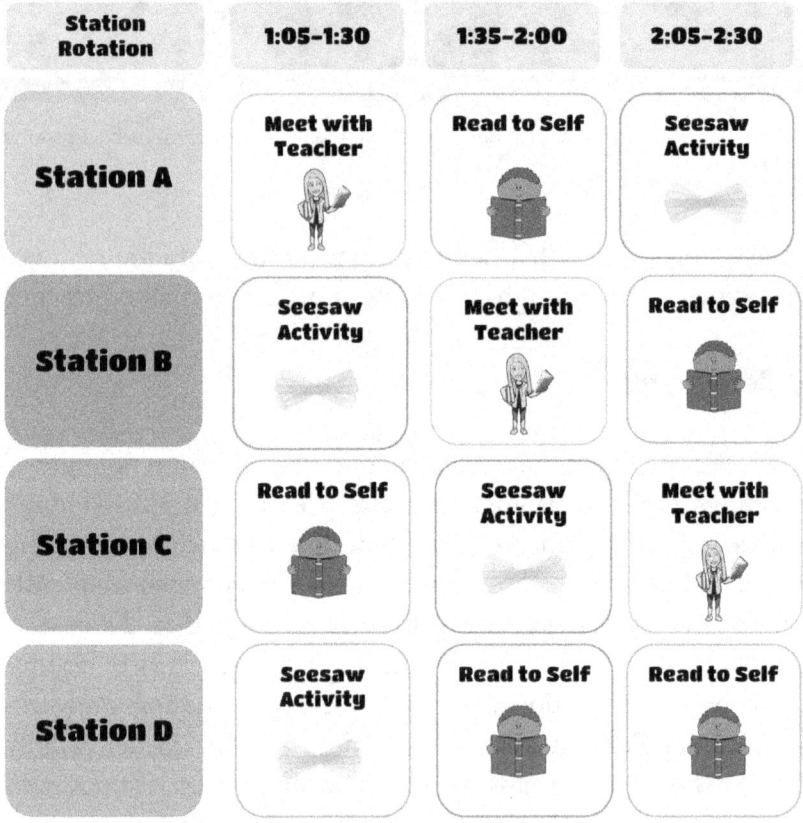

FIGURE 7.3 Grade 5: Sample guided reading stations

teacher with their own materials (chew). With student cameras pointed at their work area, the teacher then gives the students a standards-based task to complete as a group in which students can get support from peers (chew continued). As the students are working, the teacher is collecting formative data to determine which students are able to use a ten frame to make the number 10 and which students might need some additional support. Based on data they collected during the lesson, the teacher will adjust small group composition, keeping those that need additional support before they complete independent practice. All students then practice the skill in their Seesaw lesson independently that day and review it during activities in the days following (review).

> **Spotlight on Practice: Leading Live Instruction with Upper Elementary Students**

Kristin Bellinger, New Code Academy, Fourth Grade Teacher

Teaching upper elementary students online wasn't harder; it wasn't easier; it was just different. Early on I wanted to make sure my students had a routine. They needed to know what to expect and what a day in our virtual classroom looks like. Once our routine was in place, students became more independent, transition time decreased, and there was more time for learning, community building, and creativity.

I quickly realized I needed to approach our online classroom in a way that felt familiar to the students. Rather than having various scheduled meets throughout the day, we shifted to staying in the same meeting the majority of the day. During times where students were working independently, many would choose to remain in the meet and leave their camera off and microphone muted. This allowed them to ask questions or quickly get unstuck. Having a teacher continuously present and available was key to students feeling connected to the classroom.

I used this strategy when we met with small groups as well. All students were in the main google meet working independently, usually with their camera and microphones off. I had a separate small group meet where I would be synchronously working with students. When it was time to meet with a new group of students, I did a whole class announcement, and students could switch meetings for their small group with the teacher.

Oftentimes, in between small group meetings, I would turn on my microphone and ask students in the main meeting room if anyone had any questions or needed anything. Just like in the traditional classroom, students need their teacher to check in throughout extended work times. It offered me a chance to make sure my independent students were making progress and focusing on their required tasks, just like I had previously done in a traditional classroom.

I have always been a huge proponent of creating a positive class community. I was determined to make sure my students got the same opportunities to socialize, collaborate, and build community in the virtual setting. We did "get to know you" activities, had small group time, and even played games in breakout rooms. My students knew each other well, laughed together, and were a community. We had our inside jokes, talked about our lives outside of school, and some of them, even now, continue to check in on our class group chat from our 2020–2021 school year together. Synchronous meets allowed us to be engaged and successful as a virtual class.

Here are my top five tips for teaching upper elementary students through synchronous meets:

1. **Teach them to use the chat early.** Kids have a lot to share and allowing them to type it in the chat was a great way for them to share without interrupting what we were doing.
2. **Routine, routine, routine.** Find your daily routine early, stick to it, and adjust as necessary
3. **Use breakout rooms.** Breakout rooms are a great way for the kids to collaborate, socialize, play games, and build relationships with their teacher and peers.

4. **Incorporate ways for students to share about themselves.** We shared a lot of laughs during "scavenger hunt," where I would give students a category, and they would hurry to go find something to show the class. For example "find something that makes you smile."
5. **Encourage students and families to create a learning space at home.** Students who had a consistent work space, their device charger, and some sort of work surface were much more focused for synchronous meetings.

Cameras

The NCA elementary program requests that students have cameras on during live meetings. The staff has discussed camera use extensively and believe that cameras on supports the goal of building classroom communities and reading facial expressions—which is an important social skill for elementary students. Frequently used formative feedback methods for teachers, like holding up whiteboards or responding to prompts with routine hand gestures, are made possible by students having cameras on. Particularly at the upper elementary grades and NCA secondary school, having cameras off has led to less interaction with the teacher talking to a seemingly empty room—ultimately impacting the quality of instruction.

In response to emergency remote learning (ERT), a debate arose as to whether cameras should be required due to student privacy, equity, and anxiety concerns. It is important to differentiate ERT and fully online schools as families have chosen NCA's program because of its model, which includes a significant number of live class meetings each day and community as a core tenet. NCA elementary teachers communicate this expectation during "meet the teacher conferences" and ask students and families to share if there are any reasons why this expectation might not work for their family. If there are concerns, teachers have helped families troubleshoot by providing physical backgrounds, teaching how to use the green screen backgrounds within Google Meets, and utilized the social worker to get additional technology that can block out background noise. There are times when cameras are not necessary or a student just wants to take a break from being on camera. If students consistently choose not to turn their cameras on, teachers follow up to see if there is anything they need to feel more comfortable, rather than taking a punitive stance.

Live instruction through synchronous meetings is a programmatic element that seems to differentiate NCA from some other online schools. The social learning opportunities and the structure it provides for K-5 learners has proven to be an important component of NCA's program design. Many research based learning strategies such as guided practice, gradual release, differentiation, relationship building, social and emotional learning development, and movement take place during live instruction. Additionally, the pressures of ensuring that online education is successful for elementary learners prompted NCA teachers to be hyper-intentional and reflective about live instruction as there are less minutes and meetings than a brick-and-mortar classroom.

NCA's approach leads to less flexibility for students and families who need a schedule that requires less synchronous experiences. Through surveys and communication with current parents, teachers, and students there has been a variety of feedback perspectives, as some would like more synchronous time and few would prefer less. However, almost every prospective parent enrolling from other districts or online schools are seeking more synchronous learning time. NCA teachers and instructional leaders believe that live class meetings are netting great academic results and align with the core tenets of the program. NCA teachers, who all came from the brick-and-mortar classroom, cannot imagine leading elementary online learning without it.

Questions to Consider:

- How might live, synchronous class sessions align or misalign with the goals and tenets of your program?
- What type of shared experiences would you like students to have throughout the day?
- If you do not lead live instruction, how can you design opportunities for students to engage in learning together, asynchronously?
- What needs to look different when leading live class online vs. brick-and-mortar?
- How might you coach and grow your teachers in leading active, participatory, multimodal, personal, and varied live instruction?
- What will your program's policy on cameras be? What might be the impact of that policy on students or teachers?

References

Fisher, D., & Frey, N. (2013). *Better learning through structured teaching: A framework for the gradual release of responsibility.* ASCD.

Hammond, Z. (2015). *Culturally responsive teaching and the brain: Promoting authentic engagement and rigor among culturally and linguistically diverse students.* Corwin Press.

8

Designing Effective Asynchronous Instruction

This chapter will overview the affordances and constraints of designing and assigning asynchronous or independent learning activities to K-5 learners. NCA's learning management system Seesaw will be described as well as five design considerations that guided lesson creation.

One of the biggest differences between traditional brick-and-mortar school and online education is the independent or asynchronous instruction and the amount of time it takes to design. Particularly with young learners who are non- or early readers, delivering instruction and asking students to complete activities independently online requires a multifaceted approach. When designing the school, NCA instructional leaders reviewed some of the pre-built, purchasable online learning platforms but decided the design was impersonal, lacked learning elements that would motivate elementary students, and would have been difficult to navigate for primary and emergent-reading students.

Prior to launching NCA, the school district had a Seesaw for Schools (a paid version of Seesaw with additional features) subscription for all students in kindergarten through fifth grade. The digital learning team and technology integrationists had been leading professional development on Seesaw for years to provide a blended learning experience for brick-and-mortar students. Generally this looked like teachers assigning one Seesaw activity per day, usually for extra practice and/or in a station rotation model. Seesaw was chosen for NCA's independent learning platform because the teachers were familiar with the tool, it has intuitive navigation, it does not require students to know how to read, lessons are easy to build, and the administrative functions allow teachers to easily see what students have completed.

The shift for NCA teachers from using Seesaw once a day for practice activities, to depending on the platform for organization of all student assignments, communication with parents, formative feedback, and as a portion of the students' daily instruction was big. Seesaw was now the central hub for the virtual classroom and, in essence, an extension of that teacher as they built and curated the activities. In-effect, students completing online lessons designed by the teacher while the teacher is leading small group instruction puts that educator in two places at once. The design of the independent work needs to be simple and accessible as the teacher is not generally available to answer questions.

Spotlight on Practice: Designing Accessible and Effective Independent Learning Activities

Lisa Cogswell, New Code Academy, Second Grade Teacher

Building independent lessons through Seesaw allows teachers to be in two places at one time. While I am meeting with small groups, my students are being guided through independent learning activities with instructional and review videos created by myself and my teaching team. It took trial and error for my team to figure out a sustainable workflow, strategies, and the right blend of tools for making these lessons. Keeping the design consistent and simple became the best formula for our team and our students.

For each block of independent learning time, students have one assignment with multiple tasks to complete. To keep things visually consistent and simple, we use the same Google Slides template every day. Each day of the week has a specific color which is indicated at the top of the slide, with the day of the week, the subject, and a number indicating what activity it is. Each lesson begins with an introductory slide that has a numbered list of the day's tasks. For design ease, we have commonly used shapes and icons saved within the margins of our template to copy and paste quickly onto the slides.

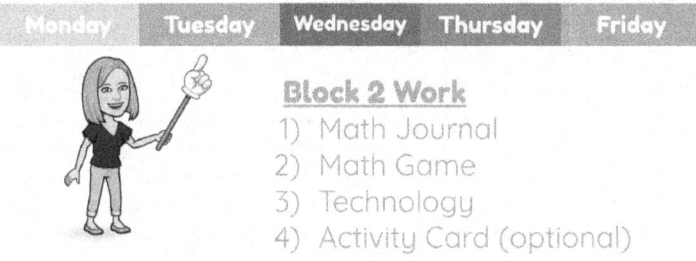

FIGURE 8.1 Grade 2: Introductory lesson slide

We keep the language on the slide simple and focused on the directions of the activities. See example below:

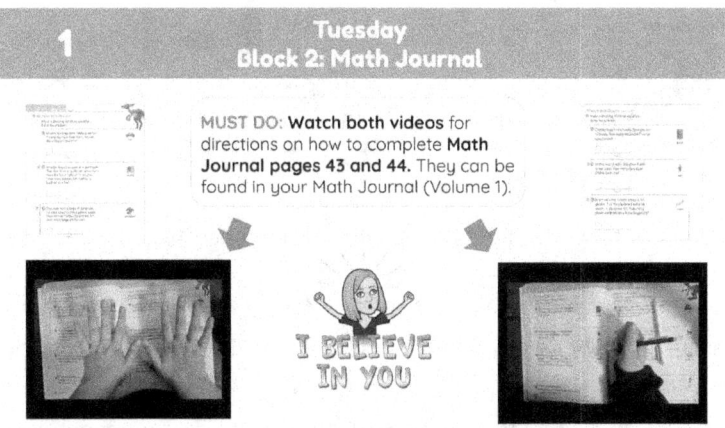

FIGURE 8.2 Adding accessibilities features in Seesaw

Every activity has multi-modal instructions. If students are completing math journal pages, we add screenshots of those specific pages to the slide for reference. The slides are then uploaded into a Seesaw activity where we record and embed multimedia elements. Any text on the slides is also saved as an audio clip so students can have the directions read to them. Additionally, we embed mini-lesson videos recorded by our team using a document camera in the slide that read the math problems and provide helpful hints.

On a new slide within the activity, directions guide students to take a picture of their completed math work and submit it. To avoid blurry pictures, we practice this skill in the first 20 days.

Other tasks within the independent work assignment include playing a math card game, which is again supported by a teacher video overview recorded using a document camera. Their task with the math game is to verbally record how playing the game went or submit a photo.

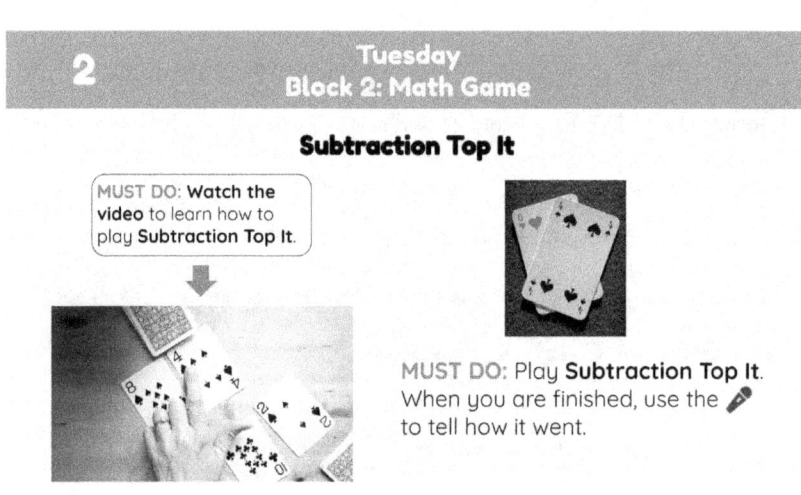

FIGURE 8.3 Math game instructions with teacher video

Additionally, students were asked to practice for 10 minutes on IXL, a standards-based learning tool that I use to differentiate activities and receive progress data on specific students.

Within the activity slide on Seesaw, I provide the directions, the link to IXL, a screenshot with sign-in instructions, and a 10-minute timer video embedded from YouTube. We strive for each independent assignment to be clear, consistent, accessible, and to give students a variety of different virtual and screen-free opportunities to practice.

Developing and saving our slides and videos in Google Drive allows us to stay organized and easily re-use our created media. Having a consistent model for what each independent learning activity should include allowed our team to split the time-consuming lesson design work. Additionally, this approach allows students to pause and rewatch the videos for extra support if they are having trouble or get feedback from me to redo a problem. I use submitted work on Seesaw to differentiate my small group math or reteach concepts to students.

Within a content block, a student will experience a whole group live lesson, a differentiated small group live lesson, and a series of independent activities to practice their new knowledge or skills. In designing independent learning activities the following considerations guided NCA teachers: 1) consistent routines, 2) types of learning activities, 3) lesson design 4) accessibility, and 5) providing feedback.

Consistent Routines

As described in Chapter 4, students participate in whole-group live lessons in the morning and afternoon followed by time to complete independent learning activities while the teacher leads small group lessons. At the end of each whole group live lesson, the teacher will overview what is assigned in Seesaw. Generally this includes the teacher sharing their screen, previewing activities, and pausing for any questions or needs. Some teachers keep the main class meeting open while meeting with small groups in a breakout room so that students who are working on their independent lessons can ask their peers questions if needed.

130 ♦ Designing Effective Asynchronous Instruction

Seesaw is the central spot for students to navigate their independent work, even if the lesson requires students to go to another website for math practice or do something that is screen-free; the directions are always housed in Seesaw. The affordances of the Seesaw student dashboard keep the students organized, manage their progress, and add features for teacher and social presence. Seesaw calls any student work assigned by teachers "Activities." When students log into their Seesaw, they click on their activities symbol which will have a red notification symbol letting them know how many assignments they need to complete or if they have teacher feedback from a previous assignment they need to read or watch. This simple navigation as well as the presence or the absence of the red notification are helpful for the students to keep track of what they need to do. Additionally, once they submit the activity for the day it disappears from their activity tab screen and that absence in the feed is a concrete sign to students they have submitted all assigned independent work.

Teachers are also afforded a user-friendly dashboard that allows them to quickly see which students have submitted the work and access individual student assignments to provide feedback. There is also a grade book to easily track points or

FIGURE 8.4 Student view when logged into Seesaw

FIGURE 8.5 Teacher view when logged into Seesaw and viewing progress

completion on activities or individual standards. All teacher created assignments are stored in a central library and can be shared with colleagues or all Seesaw users across the world. Teachers can assign lessons to the full class or differentiate which lessons are assigned to which students.

Types of Independent Work

One of the goals of independent work is to provide students with multiple approaches to practice and show progress with concepts and skills. Seesaw has a variety of tools teachers and students can use including type, draw, record a video, record a screencast, copy/paste images, drag and drop elements, record their voice, take a picture and upload, or a combination of those features. Seesaw as a platform provides students many modes of creation to show learning. For example, an activity could include a list of sight words and ask students to practice reading the words and then record themselves reading when they feel confident. Another common activity is for students to drag and drop a bank of labels to different columns such as the three branches of government or traits of different biomes. A more complex activity could include a video that extends the live lesson and asks students to reflect using developed prompts through typing or recording their thoughts.

Independent work time provides the most opportunities for screen-free student tasks throughout the day. In its simplest form, this could be students completing pages from their math workbook, reading individually, or completing the daily journal writing prompt and uploading a picture of their work. More creative offline activities could be creating the letters of vocab words out of pipe cleaners, building a pattern using items from around the house, programming their computer science robot, creating a hat and testing its softness and strength, interviewing family members, writing songs, or representing the phases of the moon with Oreos. Additionally, teachers like to provide students with a choice for their modality when possible. For instance during an activity where students develop a prototype of their invention, they can draw this using paper, their physical whiteboard, or using the Seesaw tools. Having a strong plan for materials and distribution creates more opportunities for screen-free work.

Seesaw provides the opportunity for students to talk through their thinking and demonstrate their knowledge even if they are doing a majority of their work offline. For instance, after a writing journal assignment or read to self students might be asked to record themselves reading what they wrote or their favorite passage they read from their book. Additionally with math, students might show how they solve a math problem through a screen recording where they move one, tens, and hundreds cubes. These opportunities to complete performance tasks often drive students to practice or redo their recording until they are content with their work. Teachers also embed links to websites such as Epic and IXL that are built for independent reading and practice that provide formative data to teachers on student progress of skills.

Lesson Creation

Teachers were spending a lot of time building Seesaw activities at the beginning of the year. They were perfecting the aesthetics of the slides, visuals, and videos within the activities and this effort was something they needed to simplify. To improve efficiency of lesson building, NCA teachers have built a bank of slides with commonly used graphics in a digital folder to use and build quickly. Some teachers choose to build slides in Google prior and import into Seesaw, and others build their slide pages right in Seesaw. In addition to streamlining lesson creation of slides, the amount of graphic images or design features that are unrelated to the lesson add to the cognitive load students' brains are processing while completing assignments. The media on the slides should either serve to scaffold the instructions or add a personal touch to the activity; a commonly used graphic is a Bitmoji of the teacher. Using clear and concise instructions and clutter-free slides supports students during independent work.

Videos were another element of lesson design that was taking an unsustainable amount of time for teachers to create. In addition to NCA teachers having high standards for themselves, social media video culture and the new added pressure of knowing parents would also see the videos made the creation seem more high stakes. Over time, the teachers released the pressure of making every video a production by not starting over if they made a mistake, keeping the message concise, and becoming more comfortable with students and families. Teachers also built efficiency by delegating video creation responsibilities between grade-level teammates, for instance one teacher may record the math videos for one unit or one month and then switch. The teams create a library of saved videos within a spreadsheet to be easily accessed and used again or even recording parts of a live lesson or mini lesson so that students could rewatch.

Videos are valuable because it affords students the opportunity to pause, rewatch, and show their families if they need help.

Research on educational videos indicates that videos should be 6 minutes or less for adults; children have an even shorter attention span (Brame, 2015; Guo et al., 2014). Additional suggestions supported by research on cognition include highlighting important information through text or symbols, only introducing small chunks of information, excluding anything not related to the learning goal and using multiple modalities (Brame, 2015). The video should be personable through using conversational language that is quick and enthusiastic and when possible to show the speaker's face (Brame, 2015).

> **Spotlight on Practice:**
> **The Best Tool at Your Disposal**
> **Is Knowing Your Kids**

Emily Wahlquist, New Code Academy, Third Grade Teacher

The first few weeks of our independent lessons were a flop because we were still getting to know our students' personalities and interests. We didn't know our kids all that well. We ended up having a group of students who really loved being creative, and we saw big engagement when our independent lessons asked students to represent their learning with songs, drawings, and creations.

Another engagement strategy is personalizing asynchronous work by featuring the teacher. We found that if our teacher faces were in the videos, students seemed to focus on the learning out of habit. I am a very theatrical person by nature so I brought in puppets, bitmojis of me and my grade-level colleagues on sticks, or I demonstrated a game using two stuffed animals—which was a hit with students. I also made up a song for almost everything by replacing words to music like Twinkle Twinkle Little Star to teach order of operations and PEMDAS.

Our asynchronous work in Seesaw was always connected to what we were learning in the live lessons but there never was new content. If we had been talking about recounting a text the previous two days then the asynchronous work would be rereading a book we read together with directions for students to pause at specific points and recount what they just read through voice or drawing. Same skill, but just a different way to practice. We made it a point to have all of our lessons follow a pattern so that students knew what to expect and could be successful.

Asynchronous Reading Work
1. Quick video that reviewed the standard and modeled the concept with a visual
2. Word study lesson connecting to content
3. Student activity to share about their independent reading book

Asynchronous Math Work
1. Short video reviewing the skill or strategy
2. Students complete math journal pages and post a picture of their work
3. Student complete an exit ticket for self-assessment of the skill

We learned a few things throughout the year that became common practice within our Seesaw lessons related to the ignite, chunk, chew, and review approach (Hammond, 2015):

- **Ignite with inquiry:** If you present concepts related to comprehension, students will be more engaged. For instance, starting by asking the question, "How do you know when you've understood a story?" draws the students into the concept by considering their own thinking.
- **Don't overshoot the chunk:** We initially were expecting more than what students had capacity for and that was a learning curve for us. In person, I would have assigned a whole math page, but we learned that assigning only the odd numbers still gave students plenty of practice and gave me insight into what they knew.
- **Chew what makes you happy:** Giving the most basic level of choice is fun for the kids. "Can I use the rainbow crayon in

Seesaw for this?"—Yeah go for it! It is practice for them, not for us so the more engagement and choice, the better. We noticed students gave more effort when provided a choice of process in how they showed their work.
- **Readable and relatable review:** At the beginning of the year I was trying to make everything pretty. It is more important for the design to be readable and relatable. Function is much more important than style. Audio recordings for all text was huge for some kids. Having dictated text and not having it be a big deal that your assignment is different than everyone else's mattered, and it fostered independence. I would hear from families who previously struggled in distance learning that their child didn't seem lost at all.

Accessibility

Accessibility at New Code Academy elementary includes ensuring that non-readers and students who have emerging English language skills are able to understand the directions, that teachers are using Universal Design for Learning framework to design access points to the content, and that students are provided adaptive technology when needed. Teachers make adaptations to serve the students in front of them, and thus instructional approaches and strategies can adjust from year to year. This has included working with the district adaptive technology team to provide a student who is partially blind a larger device to increase the size of print and using web browser high contrast color and zoom features.

Seesaw affords the design of accessible slides and activity instructions as teachers can use text, symbols, video, and audio to provide instructions and examples through multiple modalities. Teachers are coached to break every activity into numbered and simple steps that use the Seesaw symbols for draw, type, or

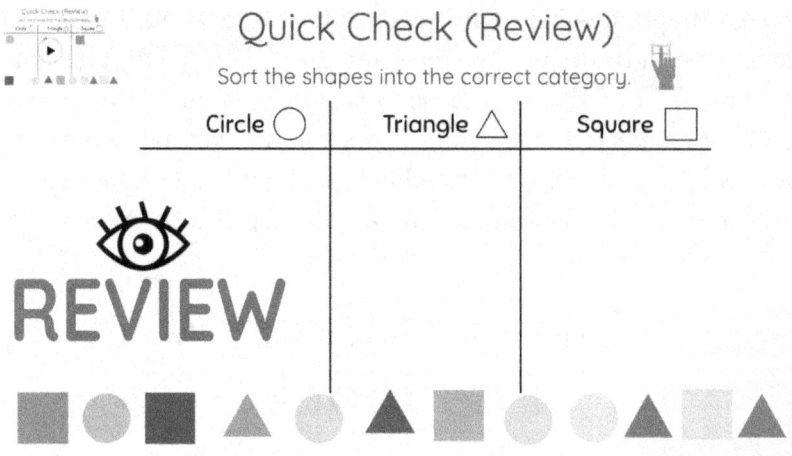

FIGURE 8.6 Slide from a Seesaw activity with a recording of the teacher modeling the activity in the upper left corner

record and then also record an audio version of those instructions. Teachers will screen record or video record themselves modeling a new activity and then embed that video right into the slide for students to reference, and Seesaw has built-in closed captioning capabilities in multiple languages within their video tool. Learning coaches have communicated that their children having access to audio and video directions has increased their independence as some needed constant adult support to read and make sense of text-based worksheet homework when they were in brick-and-mortar school. Seesaw's continued goal is compliance with Web Content Accessibility Guidelines (WCAG) 2.1 AA Standards.

Feedback

Effective feedback has been proven to have a significant positive impact on student learning and achievement (Hattie, 2012; Waack, n.d.). Furthermore, Hattie and Timperley (2007) outline that feedback is focused on the task (the learning objective), the process (the strategies or approaches the student used to get to the learning objective), and the students' self-regulation (incorporating past feedback and self-checking), rather than praise that isn't connected to learning (Waack, n.d.). Not every piece of independent student work needs to be given individual teacher feedback as a lot of the assignments are practice. A majority

Types of Seesaw Feedback

 Mrs. Skadsem

HEART
A heart means I saw your work! Thank you for completing the task.

 Mrs. Skadsem Wow! Fantastic job identify both a rectangle and a circle in your home!

Mrs. Skadsem recorded an audio comment.

COMMENT OR EDIT ITEM
If I leave a text or audio comment or edit your item, there is feedback I want to give you and I'd like you to read and listen to it!

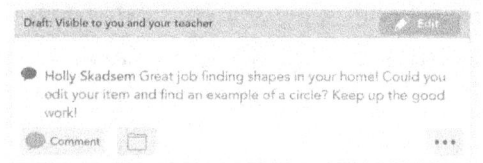

SEND BACK DRAFT
If I ask you to edit your item, please look for my teacher comment that gives you a few more steps to complete your learning process.

BLOG
I'm proud of your "WOW WORK" and it belongs on our class blog.

FIGURE 8.7 Types of feedback for students in Seesaw

of independent work within the program model is housed in Seesaw as well as a significant portion of feedback for students. Additionally, feedback to students is different from formative assessment as feedback is for the students to grow academically, and formative assessment is for the teacher to adapt and design instruction, interventions, and groupings.

Spotlight on Practice: Using Different Feedback Loops for Student Academic and Social-Emotional Growth

Emilee Vlasin, New Code Academy, Third Grade Teacher

Providing feedback online requires more planning and intention as the students are completing a lot of their work in spaces where you are not physically present. There are several ways to give feedback online, and I choose my approach based on the student's style and the feedback needed.

Asynchronous feedback through Seesaw: Feedback can be given on students' work within the platform they learn and complete independent activities through voice, video, or text. A benefit of this approach is that their families can also see this feedback and can understand their students' needs in the context of the assignment. A drawback of this approach is how much time it takes to create this feedback and the chance the student will miss it or not understand my feedback.

Feedback through one-on-one conferences: I take the last half hour of my day to conduct one-on-one meetings with students for 15 minutes each while my other students complete independent assignments. Through this approach I am able to meet with students about every two weeks, and we use the time for immediate feedback or discussion of long-term goals. The student and I look at a recent activity they did and we discuss the work rather than one-way feedback from the teacher. A benefit of this approach is the ability to provide just-in-time feedback or support and build relationships with each student.

A drawback of this approach is balancing the different needs for 1:1 meetings and scheduling accordingly.

Feedback through whole group meetings: If I am noticing quite a few students struggling with a concept we will cover it in whole class or small group meetings. For instance, there was a reader's response activity that not all were completing to their potential. In a whole class meeting I brought up a few students' work that were doing great and asked the class, "What do we see that is outstanding?" The students were then able to identify elements such as the useful sentences and connections to self they could use in their work. The benefit of this approach is being able to communicate information to more students and reducing the time it takes to provide feedback. The drawback is that the feedback does not apply to some of the students in the meeting.

Feedback through families: Families have a different role in elementary online learning, and we as teachers depend on them to be engaged in their child's education and know opportunities for academic or social-emotional growth. Sometimes families ask for feedback or extra help for their child if they notice them struggling with a concept. The benefit of this approach is that families can follow up and provide extra support to students. The drawback is that it requires vulnerability from both the teacher and the families to engage in a learning partnership and not every family has the same capacity to support.

I recommend a mixture of the feedback loops above to provide students with opportunities to gain insight on their work with their teacher, peers, family, and self-reflection.

A Note About Time

It is important to circle back to a thread found throughout this book that time works differently in online learning. The cornerstones of asynchronous learning outlined above take more time—particularly because the teacher is in two places at once, and both of those places (whether live meetings or independent work) require a lot to be created and communicated digitally. There is more media, slides, multimodal instructions, and feedback that must be delivered through technology and non-negotiable accessibility requirements. Additionally, given the physical material aspect of NCA's program, a lot of these independent activities need to be designed far in advance.

Asynchronous or independent learning activities are a central component of K-12 online learning. Particularly because many programs are predominantly asynchronous with minimal or no live class meetings. There are affordances and constraints of both purchasing the curriculum and/or platforms from a company versus teachers creating the content and multimedia. NCA teachers have shared that creating these independent learning activities provides them with more professional autonomy, supports the interdisciplinary curriculum, and creates more opportunities for both the teacher and student to add their personality to the lesson.

While it takes longer to design, it also creates efficiencies and organization on the teacher end to see who has submitted their assignment, view a digital grade book, have more opportunities for students to show what they know, and have access to data from practice platforms. The use of these tools needs to be intentional through routines, types of independent learning activities, design and accessibility, and providing feedback. NCA teachers who went from using some technology in the classroom to teaching online and immersing themselves in the affordances the technology provides, often say they could never go back to not using these tools, even in the brick-and-mortar classroom.

Questions to Consider:

- What learning platforms or apps do your teachers already use or love that could serve as your online learning hub?
- What accessibility features need to be available in your online learning hub to support the needs and styles of different learners?
- What lesson design, instructional feedback, and assessment literacies do teachers have and what professional development may be needed?

- What are hacks and templates teachers can use to make the design and building of independent learning?
- How could teachers work collaboratively to reduce the amount of creation of independent work?
- How much and what type of work should your learners experience daily and weekly?

References

Brame, C. J. (2015). *Effective educational videos.* Vanderbilt University. http://cft.vanderbilt.edu/guides-sub-pages/effective-educational-videos/

Guo, P. J., Kim, J., & Rubin, R. (2014, March). How video production affects student engagement: An empirical study of MOOC videos. In *Proceedings of the first ACM conference on Learning@scale conference* (pp. 41–50). ACM.

Hammond, Z. (2015). *Culturally responsive teaching and the brain: Promoting authentic engagement and rigor among culturally and linguistically diverse students.* Corwin Press.

Hattie, J. (2012). *Visible learning for teachers: Maximizing impact on learning.* Routledge.

Hattie, J., & Timperley, H. (2007). The power of feedback. *Review of Educational Research, 77*(1), 81–112.

Waack, S. (n.d.). Glossary of Hattie's influences on student achievement. In *Visible learning.* https://visible-learning.org/glossary/#10_Feedback

9
Fostering a Home-to-School Connection

Learning coaches are the primary caregiver(s) of New Code Academy students during school hours and support students in participating in online school. The following chapter will describe the responsibilities of learning coaches, how NCA communicates with learning coaches and families, and strategies used to build family involvement.

The world-wide shift to emergency distance learning had both positive and negative impacts on the perceptions of online education. While it illuminated a learning modality that some students found success in, it also exposed a lot of families to distance education experiences that were not effective because school systems were not prepared for such a fast and massive switch. In addition to the mental, economical, and societal stress for families during "unprecedented times," emergency remote teaching forced many parents to serve as co-teachers and put a smear on what it means to learn online. Teachers, who were being held up as heroes during the spring of 2020, were being downcast on social media by the fall of 2020 because parents felt they were essentially homeschooling their children. In contrast to ERT, elementary online learning is a family commitment; however, it should not resemble homeschooling where the parent is teaching the child.

Learning Coach

All elementary online students need a physically present adult to provide for their basic needs including food, safety, and affection. Also, K-5 students are still developing executive functioning and self-regulation skills and need support to remember meeting times and stay on task with independent work. Just as teachers participate in professional development and students gain skills and routines through the first 20 days unit, families and caregivers also need clear expectations and strategies to support their children who are learning online. NCA adopted the term "learning coach" for the primary caregiver(s) of students Monday through Friday during school hours (Waters, 2012). NCA has students who participate in school from a childcare center, their grandparents house, or at their parents' work. There are also students who have divorced parents and split their time between different homes. In these instances, a student might have more than one learning coach, and teachers copy multiple people on each communication to caregivers and families.

NCA communicates explicitly that "the best thing you can do to help your student transition to online education is to maintain your role as caregiver." Learning coaches need to remain the loving and supportive caregivers that children need, and students' relationships with caregivers should not revolve around school. Similar to families with students in physical schools, online families should be in communication with the teacher, be aware of their child's assignments, and help to build self-regulation strategies. If the learning environment is resulting in the learning coach constantly needing to be involved, there must to be an adjustment in how instruction is happening from the teacher, additional digital and independent learning skill building for the student, and/or a guidance for the learning coach on how to take a step back. NCA's approach to this is through clear communication of roles and expectations, relationship building with families and learning coaches, and ongoing family education.

Expectations for NCA Learning Coaches are:

- **Communication:** Engage in two-way communication with the teacher and school through messaging, email, or phone calls.
- **Routine:** Help the child establish and maintain a daily routine including getting ready, eating breakfast, navigating their schedule, taking breaks, and checking out of school at the end of the day.
- **Screen-free breaks:** Encourage the child to take screen-free breaks and play outside.
- **Organization:** Help the child stay organized both in their physical and digital environments. Setting up a space for learning creates a boundary between home and school as well as signals to your child's brain when it is time to learn.
- **Motivate:** Help motivate the child in their new learning environment. Set high expectations and celebrate successes. Knowing that someone cares motivates your child.
- **Frequent check-ins:** Ask the child what their schedule looks like for the day and check in about their school work.

Spotlight on Practice: A Nana's Journey as a Learning Coach and Advocate

Elizabeth Gomes Nana of New Code Academy Third Graderi

Due to devastating life circumstances, at 15 months my wife and her daughter took on full legal custody of my great-grandson T. Due to trauma, he suffers panic attacks and crippling shyness which can result in him becoming unresponsive and shutting down for hours. Brick-and-mortar kindergarten was a difficult transition, and T slowly developed a relationship with his teacher and classmates and developed a routine. The next year in first grade, his progress was disrupted as the district teachers went on strike followed by the world being locked down due to COVID-19 resulting in no structure for the second half of first grade.

As a multi-generational household, we were terrified and lost as to how to keep him safe while still ensuring he was getting what he needed developmentally. His second grade year began with distance learning and the experience was impersonal, not appropriate for second graders, and not helpful for his social or learning development. Luckily I am a retired master teacher and could support him with reading and math but I was worried how far behind he would be after this experience. However, T is unlike any kid I have ever taught or raised; he found an outlet in creating content on TikTok and has hundreds of followers. It is like pulling teeth to get him to read a picture book with me, but he taught himself to read online instructions for games he likes and reads multisyllabic words with ease.

Our local school district did not offer a distance learning option for his third grade year (2021–2022), and we were not ready to send him to brick-and-mortar school before he was vaccinated. I started to look for online options, and the research led me into a few different directions and dead ends but ultimately I found New Code Academy. What struck me about this program was the number of synchronous learning hours, opportunities to socialize in small groups with kids his age, and access to specialists. Then I discovered NCA's focus on computer science (new as of 2021–2022), and I knew I'd found my unique great-grandkid a learning home.

The transition to NCA has produced visible changes in T. At first he was resistant to keeping his camera on, but by the end of the second week he was raising his hand and participating. He likes his teachers, has settled into a routine, and connects with peers in breakout rooms. The curriculum is far more rigorous than his previous experience in distance learning. It has been a transition for me too. Since the middle of first grade my role as a learning coach had been to hover and take charge of his lessons. I started our year at NCA doing the same but I realized by doing so, T expected me to be responsible for his learning. So, I did the near impossible for a retired-teacher-cum-Nana: I backed off.

By the middle of October, T had taken over responsibility for his education by getting himself up, attending class time, listening to instructions, and preparing his workspace. He disappears every morning like he is leaving for brick-and-mortar school. And because I'm not his "teacher" anymore, I don't even get to check his work before he turns it in . . . just like in a regular classroom. Additionally, the use of electronic media to recreate real world experiences through music, art, physical education, and especially computer science has stimulated his creativity. These talented teachers have brought out the learner, experimenter, and artist in him. The psychological distance provided by being behind a screen allows him to feel safe enough to share what he creates.

I stopped being the overseer and taskmaster, freed to become T's educational assistant and cheerleader. Always somewhere nearby in the house, he calls me to his room to show me anything he's excited about working on. And, since he knows I value reading, he fetches me every day to listen with him as his teacher reads aloud. We can talk about what he's learning without him feeling tested. He can share his discoveries, challenges, and successes knowing he'll be lauded and applauded. After being an online student of NCA for only a few months, T is facing what each day brings on his own two feet, unafraid and eager. He is blossoming in ways I never knew he could. His potential expands with every opportunity presented to him. My precious great-grandkid is thriving. What more could a Nana ask?

Onboarding Families

To get families ready for online learning, a series of connection events and communication offerings were designed prior to school starting. Two weeks before the beginning of the school year one-hour, grade-level orientations were hosted for families. Orientation sessions introduced the staff, overviewed the daily schedule, clarified program expectations, previewed upcoming dates and information such as teacher conferences and school supplies, and provided families with an opportunity to ask questions. These orientations were then recorded and posted to the website for families who join NCA later or for reference. A few days before school begins, NCA hosts teacher family conferences. This introductory meeting establishes trust and provides a venue for families to share unique needs, circumstances, and strategies that are important for the teacher to know.

In addition to the orientation and conference, family tech sessions were hosted by NCA's technology integrationist the week before school began. These sessions built digital competencies related to the hardware, software, and communication venues that are core to the program model. This includes basic troubleshooting, navigation, and tricks to make the transition to online learning easier. It also introduced families to the technology integrationist as a resource that families can contact directly when they are experiencing any issues. For example, during the

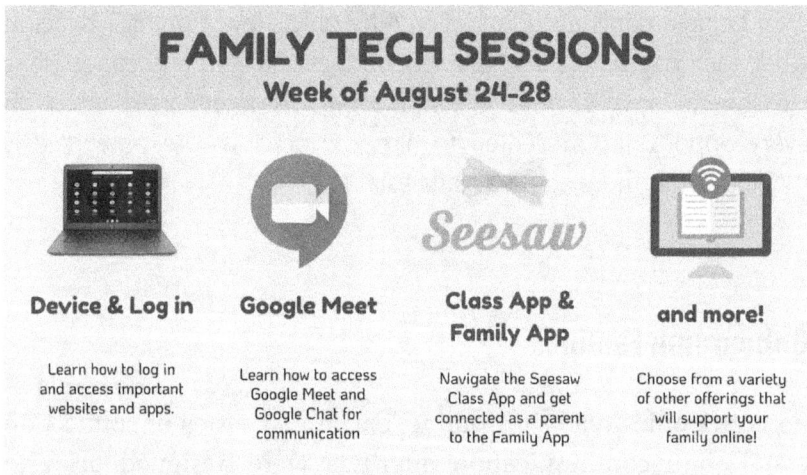

FIGURE 9.1 Family technology session offerings

first week of school, the learning coach might reach out to the technology integrationist if their student's microphone or camera isn't working to allow the teacher to keep instructing.

Communication

Clear and consistent communication has been essential for NCA, particularly as learning coaches are more involved in their student's educational experience. Information is communicated at the individual family, classroom, and school level through multiple formats. The intent is to keep families in the know without over communicating which can cause people to stop paying attention.

Student-Specific Emails and Messages

Teachers and learning coaches are regularly communicating through text via Remind (an app that allows you to text without sharing your phone number), Seesaw messages, phone calls, and email. Teachers match the communication platform to learning coach preference as well as the nature of the communication. For example, if a student is present during morning meetings and is absent for an afternoon session, a text message is most appropriate as the student may need a reminder to join the meeting.

Classroom Peek at the Week

Newsletters are also sent weekly from both the teachers and the school. The teachers send a "peek at the week" to families that share the learning objectives, any unique events and reminders, and an overview of supplies needed. Learning coaches can use the peek at the week to encourage students to organize their supplies to prepare for the next day. Teachers use a consistent visual and written summary that can be sent via Seesaw and translated to the learning coach's preferred language via Seesaw's messaging features. A script was provided to teachers that keeps language concise and consistent related to learning goals,

150 ◆ Fostering a Home-to-School Connection

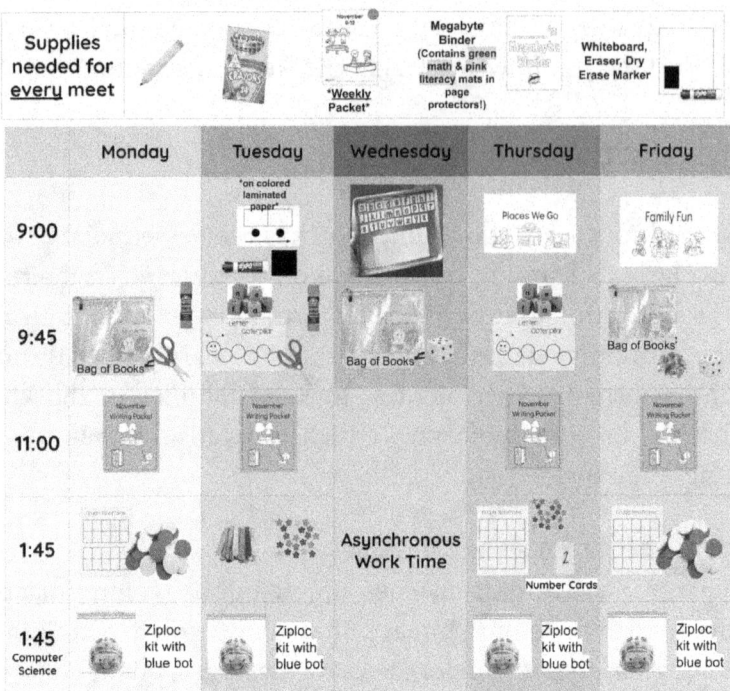

FIGURE 9.2 Kindergarten adaptation of visual "Peek at the Week"

schedule, news, and due dates and includes a visual calendar template.

Spotlight on Practice: Communication Is the Key to Working With Families in Online School

Rebecca Brower, New Code Academy, Assistant Principal K-12

Online learning is new for most of the families who attend our school and requires a different level of involvement from adult learning coaches as compared to involvement in brick-and-mortar schools. School leaders should plan for a variety of increased and consistent two-way communication with families. As a mother myself, I always approach communication with empathy as I know educational decisions can be confusing to navigate and keeping track of details about children's education can be a lot to manage. Below are my top four insights related to working with families from my first year as an online principal.

Families have more questions about the program: This is a new modality for families and people are finding that there is a lot of variation in online learning programs. In August of 2020 and 2021, our school team fielded hundreds of calls from families interested in our program. While we do host information sessions and videos, many families had specific questions to ensure the program would work for their children and their expectations of school. Many of these families are taking a leap of faith into a new form of education and have valid concerns they want to process with a school representative. Plan for increased school communication through calls and emails before the school year begins.

We have expectations for our families: Our elementary model is based on the agreement that there will be an adult learning coach physically and mentally present for our students wherever they are learning from. Families and caregivers need to see themselves as playing an important role in their child's education for our model to work. If we are clear on what is expected from parents and they agree to ensure their child has a learning coach, we find this model works very well. Keeping learning coaches informed involves regular and concise communication about what is coming up, what they should prepare for, and providing a space for them to ask questions.

Families want to be engaged in the school community: Similar to brick-and-mortar schools, parents are interested in getting involved and giving back. We have families that serve on committees, plan parties, organize spirit wear, and volunteer their time. One parent has established a physics afterschool program to give students more access to science. Parents and caregivers feel connected to our school because they see what their student is doing and hear the lessons everyday—an opportunity brick-and-mortar parents do not have. Create opportunities for families to get involved and they will contribute their interests and talents.

There needs to be multiple, functioning lines of communication: Some families are more present on email, others texting, social media, video calls, phone calls, and also messaging through the learning management system. Using different mediums helps us reach different audiences and in doing so, we had to make sure that staff are monitoring these various forms of communication and know who to direct different questions to. If we expect families to read our communication and be responsive, we must also be proactive in return.

All School Weekly Newsletter

NCA sends out a weekly Friday newsletter that includes information applicable to all students and families translated into Somali and Spanish. This school newsletter includes important dates and reminders such as virtual family nights and material pick-ups, shares contact and policy information related to absences or technology needs, and always includes a learning coach section with family education to better support online learners. All newsletters are posted to the school's website for families to view previous weeks' information.

Social Media

Social media accounts are used to share excerpts from the weekly school newsletter through visual posts that learning coaches might see as they are scrolling through their Facebook or Instagram. NCA developed a weekly schedule to keep content creation simple: Monday Teacher Feature, Tuesday Tech Tip, Wednesday Wellness Reminder, Thursday Learning Coach or Brain Break Strategy, and Friday News Bytes news show episode (*see Chapter 10*). Sharing this information via social media also serves as marketing to potential families about NCA's program model and school culture.

FIGURE 9.3 Example NCA social media posts

Volunteering

Parent involvement to organize events, fundraisers, and celebrations within brick-and-mortar schools is beneficial to school culture, and online school is no different. To facilitate involvement, a parent advisory board was created and organized around program problems and solutions such as students needing more out of school time socialization which resulted in clubs and class parties. The advisory board of over 20 parents, and three teachers consists of four committees developed based on requests from parents: yearbook, class parties, community building, and family education. The work these committees do make the school community special and ensure that online learning isn't less than because students do not have access to brick-and-mortar traditions.

Spotlight on Practice: Family Contributions to Community Building

Megan Reams, Parent of Two New Code Academy Students

When the pandemic hit in 2020, I opted for online school for a consistent educational experience for my two children, and we continued in NCA the following year with the same motivations. While there were some ups and downs of the switch, overall it has been a phenomenal experience, and we feel a part of the school community. At NCA parents have an opportunity to contribute to the school community through different committees, and I was excited to participate. I knew I wanted my kids to have as many of the same experiences they had with regards to parties and community building as they did in brick-and-mortar school.

I co-led the class party committee at NCA and we planned four parties a year. All the parents were a bit nervous about what a party would look like online, but we quickly discovered it was going to be much easier than we thought. The parent volunteers received guidance on how to ensure all students felt included and created an idea repository to share across classrooms and grade levels. I also served on the teacher appreciation committee which required creative thinking as to how to recognize teachers that do not go to a physical school each day. Through donations from NCA families and the community, we showed our appreciation for all the amazing work the teachers do each day. The result was goodie bags teachers were instructed to open each day of the week to find a yard sign, snacks, gift cards, and a class-created book on all the things they love about their teacher.

Another committee I participated in was the yearbook committee. There was a big push to make sure that every child was represented in the yearbook—even if that meant their teacher took a screenshot of them in a class meeting. This struck me because in the brick-and-mortar schools, if you don't get your school photo taken you just are not in the yearbook.

The community building committee put together an online spirit wear store that was well received by all families. The kids were encouraged to wear their Megabyte wear on Fridays throughout the school year. Additionally I hosted a second grade virtual Lego club. We would do different building challenges led by the student or myself. We would all have fun playing together. The kids just needed someone to create that space to connect together, and after a few sessions, they didn't need me to do much leading.

A group of staff and parents worked to ensure the fifth graders had a special celebration of their graduation from elementary school! Staff organized the on-line ceremony, and another parent and I coordinated an brick-and-mortar opportunity for the students to meet the fifth grade teachers and specialists one at a time. It was the first time most students had an opportunity to meet their teachers and specialists in person. There was a gigantic yard sign congratulating the fifth graders, balloons, a photo frame, and a special Megabyte cupcake for each graduate.

As a parent who loves to volunteer, I appreciated the school providing opportunities for us as parents to create similar celebrations as the brick-and-mortar schools. Some volunteer opportunities were easier online and some presented logistical, but not insurmountable challenges. My participation with NCA led to engagement with my children, their teachers, and other families as we were all experiencing something new. The prioritization of equity throughout these committees motivated me as it sent the message that the school really cared about all the students. I know not all parents are able to volunteer like I am so I hope my skills and contributions created memories for all children.

Virtual Family Nights

NCA hosts virtual family nights to develop a stronger home to school connection. During these events, families indicated interest through a Google Form and are sent home supplies in the monthly material pick up. Year one themes included: reading, STEM, wellness, and BINGO and game night. Families were sent an email prior to the event with the list of things they needed (e.g. the materials sent home by the school, pencils, paper, etc.). Families were instructed to log on together, and younger siblings were encouraged to participate as well. All activities, games, etc. were differentiated knowing that family members would range in age from pre-K up to fifth grade. Family night programming included time for families to connect with other NCA families in breakout rooms through games, discussions, or group challenges. Virtual family nights have been well attended and an effective way to build community online.

Online learning provides a beautiful opportunity to create the learning partnerships between caregivers, teachers, and students that can have positive impacts on students' experiences and achievement. The COVID-19 pandemic has changed families involvement and understandings of the school system and it is a strategic moment to get caregivers more involved. Due to the development and executive functioning skills of elementary learners, caring adults need to be involved in their education but not serve as an additional teacher. It is a tricky balance and looks different for every family.

Questions to Consider:
- What do families need to know about your program design and the expectations you have for the teacher, student, and learning coach?
- What strategies and ideas can you provide learning coaches so they can support their children with learning while still giving their children opportunities to build independence?
- How can the talents, skills, and time of parents be utilized to build community and solve problems at your school?
- How can you be cognizant and empathetic to families with their questions and anxieties about switching to an online learning modality?
- What intentional ways will you collect feedback from families to improve your program?

Reference

Waters, L. H. (2012). *Exploring the experiences of learning coaches in a cyber charter school: A qualitative case study* [Doctoral dissertation, University of Hawaii] (1347666490). ProQuest Dissertation Publishing.

10

Creating a Sense of Belonging in Online School

Community is essential for elementary online learning. The following chapter describes program design and instructional strategies that intentionally build relationships in developmentally appropriate ways.

Belonging is a basic need, right after food and security according to Maslow's motivational hierarchy (Maslow, 1943). In order to feel motivated, learners need contact and communication with people who care about them and with whom they have stable relationships (Baumeister & Leary, 1995). When students feel they are part of a community that accepts and loves them for who they are, they are more engaged, contribute more effort, and experience more success (Juvonen, 2006). Particularly for young elementary learners who are newer to navigating relationships and interpersonal experiences, schools must create and nurture an environment where students can feel comfortable to engage in academics. Educators and administrators know this; however sometimes intentional and ongoing relationship building takes a back seat to academics. In online learning, that can look like more independent work and less opportunities to engage in academic or social emotional discourse with teachers and peers.

There is a stereotype that online learning is not a good fit for elementary students because they are isolated and unable to build meaningful relationships with peers and their teacher. NCA was hyper-aware of this critique and prioritized intentional community building and providing a sense of belonging for K-5 students. While community building is also a priority for brick-and-mortar schools, there are more opportunities for organic socialization including on the bus, playground, at lunch, and while working around the classroom. In online elementary school, social moments need to be built and scaffolded. Staff must first ensure students know how to use the communication tools and next help develop students' social skills to connect with peers in different spaces. All of these things can be part of an online classroom as long as the teacher intentionally created the conditions.

Circling back to the Community of Inquiry model (see Chapter 1), social presence is defined as "the degree to which learners feel socially and emotionally connected with others in an online environment" (Cleveland-Innes & Campbell, 2012, p. 272). It is not simply about giving students a chance to talk with their teacher and fellow students, but about creating a safe environment, building trust amongst community members, norms in how communication will happen so that learners know how to engage, and attention to how cognition is connected to emotions. Social presence includes the interactions between students-to-peers, students-to-teachers, students-to-content, and students-to-the-world (Vincent-Layton, n.d.). Within these interactions, students must have opportunities to bring in and share their identity and cultural perspectives as well as learn about others perspectives and beliefs. Additionally, teachers need to be cognizant of how power and status can shape who dominates conversations and how all voices can be heard (Gutiérrez, 2012).

Creating a Sense of Belonging Online ◆ 159

Daily Community Connection

Morning Meeting

To prioritize community building and create consistent opportunities for social presence every day, NCA created three non-negotiable daily class meetings focused on community. As overviewed in the program design chapter, each class begins the day with a morning meeting from 9:00–9:30 am, have a midday full class check-in, and a closing circle meeting from 3:00–3:15 pm that focuses on relationship building, reflection and sharing, and creating shared experiences. NCA instructional leaders felt there was value in designing the schedule like a school day and that meant intentional opening and closing of the day.

The term "morning meeting" is most synonymous with Responsive Classroom, which is a very specific approach to creating community, discipline, academics, and developmental awareness (www.responsiveclassroom.org). NCA is not a responsive classroom school, but does use social-emotional learning activities from the framework. Teachers have full autonomy over the structure of the meetings and the activities that take place. Morning meetings start off very structured

Morning Meeting: Greeting & Sharing

Teacher: I will pull two sticks. Those two students will unmute and ask each other about their favorite season.

Student 1: **Good morning _____. What is your favorite season?**

Student 2: **Good morning _____. My favorite season is _____. Thank you for asking. What is your favorite season?**

Student 1: **My favorite season is _____. Thank you for asking.**

FIGURE 10.1 3rd grade: Morning meeting activity slide

at the beginning of the year as teachers and students become comfortable with each other and create routines. Teachers found that once community and trust were built, the activities didn't need to be super complex to ignite powerful sharing amongst students and teachers.

The meetings generally consist of some combination of a greeting, activity, game, song, and/or small breakout rooms. The reality of an online greeting is that students take a couple of seconds to umute and interactions are not always as fluid as being in the same brick and mortar space. However, this becomes more normal over time. One strategy to make a whole group greeting more efficient is to ask students to turn off their camera after they have shared to indicate they should not be called on by their peers.

Some of NCA's favorite morning meeting activities include:

- Playing a "Guess the Animal Sound" from YouTube. Teachers play the sound then pause the video and the students either write or draw what animal they think it is on their whiteboard. After 15 seconds everyone shows their guess, the teacher unpauses the video, and the answer is revealed.
- Drawing a few names from a cup to share based on a question of the day such as "what are you going to do this weekend?" or "what did you have for breakfast?" and allowing for a few follow-up questions from peers.
- Playing a "song of the day" and picking a few lines from the lyrics to discuss as a class or in small groups.
- Playing a class detective game where one student leaves the online meeting and the teacher chooses one student to be "it." That student starts moving their body such as jumping up and down, patting their head, or scratching their face, and the whole class copies them. The detective must figure out who is leading the movements but only gets three guesses.

Midday Check-in

The midday check-in is an essential touch-point to create shared experiences and refocus students. In a brick-and-mortar school, students have more shared experiences as they move through their day doing the same thing at the same time such as waiting to drink out of the water fountain. Teachers must be intentional about creating those shared experiences during meetings and check-ins. The students may have eaten very different foods, in very different spaces, but they all ate breakfast, so inviting them to speak or type what they ate is a simple way to create shared experiences. In addition to connecting as a community, teachers realized that if you don't build in time to come back together throughout the day, you will lose the students to distractions. Five to 15-minute check-ins also create a space for the students to ask questions and the teacher to clarify directions. Students need a moment to reflect on or celebrate work they completed and spark motivation for the work ahead.

Thursday
Morning Meeting: Greeting and Sharing

Greeting and Share Time

I will split you into groups in Breakout Rooms. You will have time to **greet each other** and **talk**.

Here are some reminders for talking with others:
★ **Listen** to what others have to say without interrupting.
★ Ask each other **questions**.
★ Give **everyone a chance to talk**.
★ **Be kind**.
★ **Be school appropriate** with your words and actions.

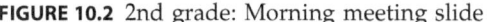

FIGURE 10.2 2nd grade: Morning meeting slide

Closing Circle

Closing circle is reserved for connecting and reflecting on the day as a whole class including celebrating all the work that was done and looking ahead to upcoming lessons. For example, one second grade classroom always chose a "star" or high point and a "wish" or a hope for tomorrow. Students love going into meeting breakout rooms with a small group of peers and friends for socialization. Whether it was for 60 seconds for a quick activity or a longer unstructured hang out with friends, students like to socialize in smaller groups with more privacy. As NCA learns in the same physical space as they live, closing the day in a meeting helps students transition out of their student mode for the night.

Spotlight on Practice: Investing Time in Social Emotional Learning and Community

Matt Marohn, New Code Academy, Fifth Grade Teacher

At the beginning of the year our staff collectively decided we would commit a half-hour at the beginning of the day to a morning meeting and 15 minutes at the end of the day for closing circle. I was a little worried when this decision was made because that is 45 minutes devoted to community building, and we were trying to balance screen time and the amount of live-class meetings. How could committing 45 minutes of our live class meetings to social-emotional learning impact the students academically? Once the school year began, I quickly realized the morning and closing meeting was essential to making the rest of the day work.

That 30 minutes of morning meeting and building those relationships seemed painful at first as the meetings were very structured and teacher-driven. As the fifth grade students and teachers all grew more comfortable with the technology and with each other, we as teachers collected feedback from the students and new activity ideas from our peers. What resulted was a more casual and social meeting that was part whole-group and part in breakout rooms as small groups. If students were in breakout rooms during morning meetings, I would pop into the different rooms to check in and find ways to connect personally.

Students had a voice and could choose in what room and activity they wanted to participate, which led to more engagement. Playing group online games such as Battleship, Bingo, and Connect 4 was a popular activity that helped students connect. My favorite game was Drawasaurus (drawasaurus.org) where one participant gets prompted to draw a word and the rest of us guess via the chat. Some of the drawings would have me laughing so hard I would have tears in my eyes.

I became more aware of how I started each day as well. My goal was always to start each morning meeting overly positive, pleasant, and happy. Sometimes I needed to pump myself up by listening to music or doing a little reading before starting the day. If I started my day frazzled or not prepared, it seemed to have an impact on my students' day. If I started that morning meeting calm, happy, and laughing; I could tell it made my students feel relaxed. I also carried this mantra throughout the day whenever a student came late to a class meeting. Sometimes the student would apologize or try to explain what happened. My response was always, "I am so glad you are here, no worries," and quickly tried to explain what we were doing.

The morning meetings and closing circles made our class a community. The relationships built in these meetings—between the students and between myself and the students—paid dividends academically. Students were more comfortable participating in class, and I had more insight on how to make the learning relevant and personal.

School-Wide Community Building

Elementary schools are known for hosting a lot of events and celebrations that encourage play, imagination, and joy. Some of the favorite community events were identified from the brick-and-mortar school and brought online.

Spirit Weeks

Spirit days or dress-up days are a big hit at the elementary level. NCA wanted to replicate this experience online as a chance to bring joy and create community. The first spirit week took place in October and was planned by the NCA social justice committee to determine themes and dress up ideas that would be inclusive and accessible. Spirit week was also the launch of NCA's school-wide Facebook and Instagram accounts. Throughout the week, the joy and excitement of spirit week was captured through screenshots and photos and posted on social media to share with families. Community grew exponentially with two small steps.

School Identity

A strategy to build belongingness was to strengthen the identity of the school through selecting a mascot and designing spirit wear. All of the brick-and-mortar elementary schools have mascots, so online school should be no exception. Classrooms were provided with three mascot ideas and given time to discuss, advocate, and vote on their favorite option. Collectively, students chose "Megabyte" the shark to represent New Code Academy. Megabyte, an inflatable shark costume, is integrated into school rallies, parties, and activities. Megabyte the shark was also featured on school spirit wear, designed by the parent advisory committee. The group created a range of options for students, staff, and families with affordability being a top priority. Students were encouraged to wear turquoise or blue on Fridays and celebrated all interpretations of this whether they wore spirit gear or not.

School Rallies

Elementary schools regularly bring the whole student body together in a large gathering space such as the gym to build

FIGURE 10.3 Megabyte spirit week days calendar communicated with families

community and collective school spirit. Online, rallies became opportunities for cross grade-level connections and a fun opportunity for students to be in an online meeting with peers from other classes. Each rally has a K-5 theme such as reading or wellness. The rallies start with the NCA school cheer and an appearance from Megabyte the school mascot, then move into a read aloud that fit the theme, and end with student choice breakout rooms. If there is an activity that requires any materials, the staff ensure it is something that students could find around the house or send materials home in the monthly materials.

One of the students' favorite spirit rallies focused on wellness. Students at each grade level started the rally by watching a Megabyte Wellness video. Megabyte demonstrated ways students could fuel their body, calm their body, and move their body. Teachers then moved into a read aloud of their choice:

- **Move your body:** *The Couch Potato* by Jory John
- **Fuel your body:** *I Will Never Not Ever Eat a Tomato* by Lauren Child

- **Calm your body:** *What Does It Mean to be Present?* by Rana DiOrio
- **Calm your body:** *I Am Peace, A Book of Mindfulness* by Susan Verde

The rally ended with student breakout room choices including mandala coloring pages, a directed draw, breathing strategies, or cosmic kids yoga.

Class Parties

As shared in Chapter 9, each classroom has a parent "room lead" who takes on the responsibility of planning four class parties for the year. The parties take place in the fall, mid-year, spring, and end of the school year, and the social justice committee ensures the dates don't align with any religious or pre-existing holidays. The parents host games, speakers, and activities via a Google Meet for the students, families, and teachers. The goals of the party, as defined by the social justice committee are to 1) build community, 2) involve families, 3) build social skills, 4) provide opportunities for collective experiences and memories,

Megabyte Cheer!

Our school name is NCA 🐙
We Care 💜
You Matter, Everyday 😎
Learning is what we do best 🧠
We'll grow so much 🌱
You'll be impressed 👍
Creators, Thinkers, Leaders too 👦
We're a team the whole way through 👯
I'm a Meg-a-byte *clap clap* 👏
We are Meg-a-bytes *chomp* 🦈

FIGURE 10.4 NCA school cheer

5) practice teamwork, 6) have fun, and 7) be in a place where students feel successful. For example, a third grad party included a collaborative virtual escape room, the Zoomed In game, where participants guess what the object is as the camera slowly zooms out, collaborative Mad Libs, and a freeze dance.

NewsBYTEs News Show

NCA's technology integrationist came up with an idea to build community across the school by launching a news show that every class watches on Friday mornings. In collaboration with a paraprofessional staff member, the two create a script and prepare a new group of fifth graders each week to be the news anchors. The anchors cover school news and announcements as well as the weather by first practicing the script together and then recording themselves. In addition to the 5th grade anchors, students and families can submit videos for joke of the week or a book review, and it is always fun to see NCA siblings together on camera. Families can submit pictures and videos to a segment called "Megabytes in the Wild" that feature students in their home environment playing in the snow, going on vacation, and spending time with loved ones.

The news show garners an enthusiastic response from students and families. Students ask the teachers if they can get their joke chosen for the news show during material pick-up, and families will email in anticipation if the news show is not uploaded by 9 am on Friday. At the end of year one there were two special news shows, the first featured kindergarteners as the anchors to honor their virtual graduation, and the second featured the fourth graders honoring the fifth graders' graduation and transition to middle school.

Creating Space for Socialization

Each week students have a mini lesson with the media specialist and social worker. Both adults try to build social-emotional skills during their time with students through book selection on how to make friends, how to appreciate differences, and how to resolve conflict. The social worker also hosts a school-wide lunch bunch for students who want to hang out with other students during their break. The social worker prompts the conversation and creates a safe space for the students to share their feelings. Another space for students to get together are clubs, for instance during year one, a group of fifth graders created a Harry Potter club with the help of a paraprofessional and parent volunteers. They organized and advertised an event for second through fifth graders to do different themed activities in breakout rooms. Staff members encouraged the club and attended the gathering.

Spotlight on Practice: Building Community Through Book Clubs

Anna Weber, New Code Academy, Fourth Grade Teacher

As we began to design the English language arts curriculum and instruction, we considered high-value activities from the brick-and-mortar classroom that could be adapted for online school. The use of book clubs has always been an engaging format for students to talk and write about what they are reading. Using critical thinking to discuss and make connections to a text as a group gives reading more purpose for students.

We introduced book clubs about half-way through the year after students became more comfortable with online tools and how to participate within meetings. Up to the mid-year point, meetings had been more formal with concrete norms on how to participate by raising your hand and staying on mute when not speaking. Book clubs challenged both the students and teachers to be a bit more fluid in our conversations and how we were engaging in online meetings. To guide the conversation, we printed out and sent home an accountable talk prompting card with sentence starters to help students agree with, disagree with, add-on to, prompt, get further explanation, and clarify with their group members. After going over how to use the card to support their discussions, we asked students to have the card present or use their digital copy during book clubs as a resource. We hoped that having the card would help scaffold student's book club conversations to be increasingly independent.

Each class was put into groups of five students based on a combination of reading level, book topic interest, and ensuring various personality types were represented in each group. Personality-wise, we needed at least one or two students who we thought would have the confidence to take on a leadership role and be willing to prompt others in the group. The groups all read high-interest books and were asked to journal independently on a Google doc shared with the teacher prior to the book club meeting. This journal prompt was meant to hold the students accountable for their reading and give them space to think about what they just read before engaging in conversation. At the start of using book clubs, we as teachers took a more dominant role in prompting and guiding conversation and overtime shifted that role to the students as they became confident and comfortable with the process.

There were some blips and not every book club meeting was perfect; however, overall the experience was of high value for students academically and social-emotionally. Academically, book clubs led to literacy-rich conversations where students made connections from self-to-text, text-to-text, text-to-others, and self-to-others. There was an excitement for book club time with less absences and more engagement in the conversation than other whole-class meetings. The autonomy students had to drive the conversation seemed to ignite the love of reading. Social-emotionally, having a consistent small group to check in with twice a week led to a more relaxed atmosphere and students willing to share about their feelings and perspectives. I noticed students being more vocal and vulnerable about their thoughts because they knew their small group and had built trust within this sub-community of the larger class.

I could see the relationships, trust, and conversation skills that grew out of book clubs transferring to other subjects and activities. Particularly, in a unit where the culminating projects had students presenting to each other about different U.S. states, the peer-to-peer small group support in designing the project as well as thoughtful prompting questions during the presentations all seemed tied to our book club experience. In the future, I would like to start book clubs earlier in the year and I am considering how to make the pre-club journal prompt collaborative.

Teacher Moves That Make a Difference

In addition to the school-wide and classroom-based activities designed to build community, there are also moment-to-moment teacher moves that communicate respect, empathy, and love to students leading to stronger learning partnerships. These moves are often small and come naturally to teachers because of their caring dispositions, but research shows that it is the everyday actions of teachers and peers that can contribute to students' sense of belonging (Bouchard & Berg, 2017).

Below is a list of caring teacher moves collected from the talented NCA educators:

- Welcoming students with a positive disposition when they are late to class
- Leaving personal feedback on their work
- Staying after class so that students can ask questions or share something they are really excited to tell someone about
- Hosting 1:1 check-in meetings with students to make a personal connection, set or review learning goals, or get feedback on their favorite/least favorite parts of school
- Identifying and intervening with student-to-student conflict to ensure the issue is resolved with all parties feeling respect

- Reaching out to families if a student is absent or missing work to ensure everything is okay and inquire how you can help the student catch up

Spotlight on Practice: Scaffolding Play to Build Authentic Connections

Allie Kalkman, New Code Academy, Kindergarten Teacher

Play is an essential part of learning in primary education. As a kindergarten teacher, I ensure that play is a protected part of my students' day in order to grow in social skills as well as encourage creativity, learning through exploration, and problem solving. Switching to an online setting, I knew that I would need to be intentional about creating time for play but also teaching students how to interact and form relationships through a screen.

While I believe that students need to play and work with all students, I wanted to be sure that each student's first play experience was with someone they felt comfortable with given this setting. I sent students a chart with everyone's picture in Seesaw and asked them to circle four friends they would like to play with. From there, I intentionally made groups of two to three students for our first play groups.

Similar to introducing academic skills, I took a scaffolded approach to play groups:

1. During the first two rounds of meetings, I began to play groups by facilitating asking questions in order for the students to get to know each other better. Questions students practiced asking and answering included, "What is your favorite toy?," "Who do you live with?," and "What did you do last night with your family?" After a few minutes of questioning each child brought a toy to play with and I acted as an active participant in the play group.

2. When students felt comfortable with that model, I joined each play group but muted myself. Students could still see that I was there; however, I only interjected if there was prolonged silence or another issue.
3. Then I joined the playgroup with both my camera and microphone off. I was there if really needed, students need time with their peers where adults do not intervene or lead, but rather are around for help if the students ask for it.
4. The final step was hosting several playgroups at a time. My microphone and camera remained off and I popped between groups but did not participate.

This scaffolded approach led students to form connections with many students over the course of a month and created lively play experiences that did not feel natural for many students at the beginning of the year. This format also helped lay the foundation for partner work in breakout rooms during literacy and math lessons. I reinforced talking with a peer during our morning meeting time by giving students a prompt and having them share their responses in several breakout rooms with a variety of their peers.

One of the happiest surprises from this past school year is the connections that my students were able to form with each other through a screen. The relationships my students formed felt just as connected as students that had been learning in the same room with each other all year. In the spring, several students ran into classmates at parks and other events. In each instance, they recognized their classmates and began playing together as friends.

Additional Recommendations:
- Encourage toys that do not make noise as it leads to less conversation between students.
- Headphones help with background noise and focus.

- Toy access is not equal and I will begin with coloring next year. My team created a toy library from community donations that families could opt-in to access.

There can be misconceptions about online learning from people outside of the school community. They may assume online learning lacks socialization and consists of a student completing a series of modules alone all day. In Chapter 9, it was shared that a student transferred to NCA due to lack of interaction in their previous online school, indicating that these online program models do exist at the elementary level. At NCA, It is the intentionality behind the social presence that makes the difference.

During the last week of school, a third grade student asked the teacher if they could stay on after the meeting when students were transitioning to end-of-day tasks. When the other students had left, the student began crying. Her teacher asked her about the emotions she was feeling. The student proceeded to explain that she was feeling so sad that school was ending and she wouldn't be able to see her friends and her teacher every day. The conversation between the teacher and student went on for about 20 minutes as they worked together to process the big feelings of the school year coming to an end.

Questions to Consider When Planning Intentional Community Building in Online Elementary Schools:
- What are social events or traditions that take place in brick-and-mortar schools that garner a lot of excitement from students?
- What are intentional ways community and relationships can be built at the school, classroom, and student-to-student or student-to-teacher level?

- What safeguards or non-negotiables are built within the online program design to ensure that community building and social-emotional learning remain a priority?
- Who are the students within the school community and what processes or committees could ensure that events and gatherings are inclusive and welcoming of all students?
- How can students be provided space to build friendships in small groups or 1:1 within an online environment?

References

Baumeister, R. F., & Leary, M. R. (1995). The need to belong: Desire for interpersonal attachments as a fundamental human motivation. *Psychological Bulletin, 117*(3), 497–529.

Bouchard, K. L., & Berg, D. H. (2017). Students' school belonging: Juxtaposing the perspectives of teachers and students in the late elementary school years (grades 4–8). *School Community Journal, 27*(1), 107–136.

Cleveland-Innes, M., & Campbell, P. (2012). Emotional presence, learning, and the online learning environment. *The International Review of Research in Open and Distributed Learning, 13*(4), 269–292.

Gutiérrez, R. (2012). Context matters: How should we conceptualize equity in mathematics education? In *Equity in discourse for mathematics education* (pp. 17–33). Springer.

Juvonen, J. (2006). Sense of belonging, social relationships, and school functioning. In P. A. Alexander & P. H. Winne (Eds.), *Handbook of educational psychology* (2nd ed., pp. 655–674). Lawrence Erlbaum.

Maslow, A. H. (1943). A theory of human motivation. *Psychological Review, 50*(4), 370–396.

Vincent-Layton, K. (n.d.). *Social presence and interaction in the online classroom*. Brigham Young University's Center for Teaching and Learning. https://ctl.byu.edu/tip/social-presence-and-interaction-online-classroom

11

Evolving and Growing

New Code Academy was launched during a moment in educational history when schools were figuring out how to navigate education day-by-day; and NCA was no exception. Contextually, the pandemic created a sense of urgency and increased online enrollments; yet, no matter what the future holds, elementary online learning is here to stay. As a summary of the information in this book, this chapter begins with recommended priorities for instructional leaders building K-5 online programs.

Priorities for Building K-5 Online Programs

Define the student experience: Before diving into the logistical program details and tasks, bring together a multi-perspective team to define what elementary students need to learn and experience each day. By identifying beliefs about learning, core program tenets, and research-based instructional frameworks first, the group can identify some non-negotiables for the student experience and design the staffing, professional development, timelines, and budgets to match.

Equity is crucial: Creating a new program is the perfect time to address educational inequities that have caused disparities in academic success. This must include growing the school team's understanding of equity and culturally responsive teaching in order to engage in critical examinations of access, achievement, identity, and power within the online school.

Prioritize community: Online learning lives in cyberspace which creates affordances and constraints for community building. Intentional relationship building with and between students, with learning coaches and families, between colleagues, and across the school community is essential for student engagement, equitable instruction, and creating a developmentally appropriate environment for students. It is easy to fall into the trap of academics eclipsing community building until it is acknowledged that the two are dependent on each other.

Seek feedback and adjust: The best-made plans for an elementary online school model will still need changes as the educational modality evolves and staff, students, and families become savvy in online pedagogy. Plan for regular data collection from the school community and be ready to adjust program design and expectations to better serve students.

Program champions: Launching an elementary online school will sometimes feel like stepping into the great unknown. Find passionate staff members who are willing to strap on a helmet and guide the rocket ship with ideas, problem solving, and a flexible mindset. As an instructional leader, create space for these program champions to contribute their skills and talents to making the program better by working in partnership.

Online is new for all: Students, teachers, and families all need training and patience as they adapt to a new learning environment. Most people have strong images of what school is, as well as their role within school. These schemas and beliefs need scaffolding on new ways of teaching, learning, and supporting online.

Don't cut corners: Students in online programs need the same access to teachers, specialists, and academic supports, as well as subjects, experiences, and resources. Developing an online school is not a chance to save money or stretch staff capacity across a higher proportion of students or work. While there will be cost savings in some areas such as facilities and transportation, there will be additional expenses related to technology and resources. Low-quality programs will result in families choosing other online schools.

Navigate the system: Creating an online program within a traditional brick-and-mortar educational system will come with growing pains. The calculations and models related to things like budgets, timelines, teacher prep minutes, curriculum and professional development do not translate between the two modalities. Instructional leaders need to create support at all levels and strategically navigate the hurdles of the system.

Spotlight on Practice: Driving Reform in a Large System

John Weisser, Executive Director of Technology & Information Services, Bloomington Public Schools

Our digital learning team is a small but mighty group of educators turned district leaders that drive innovation and coordinate all things technology for our district. From information technology, computer science education, integrating technology within classrooms, and building our online schools; our team's responsibilities range from highly technical to visioning for the future. As we looked across the changing landscape of K-12 online learning we knew we had to stay responsive to our family's feedback and establish our space in this new learning landscape.

In the spring of 2021, we used an empathy-driven design thinking approach to establish a future direction of our online school. We asked families, "What is something that draws you to the online program and what would tip the scale for you to stay beyond COVID-19?" Generally the answers were that the style worked for their student, and the school offered something the brick-and-mortar experience didn't. This led us to considering magnet-style themes for our online school including environmental education, leadership and entrepreneurship, and computer science education.

Two years prior our district had begun building a K-12 computer science pathway for students with the large goals of creating joy, equity, and transferable skills within education. It had been successful and well received in its launch and was drawing the attention of families and students. Given the financial and pedagogical investment as well as our growing expertise, it seemed to make the most sense for us to bring this focus into the online space.

As shared in Jim Collin's *Good to Great* (2001), reform within any large scale system is challenging. Creating a magnet school or options within a larger traditional school builds incentive for families to make alternative choices in a system that is built and projected based on geographic boundaries. Whenever you add a disruption that draws students from one side of the district to the other or online, it could be perceived as a threat even though these programs tend to draw students in from outside of district—which benefits the system as a whole. However, our enrollment trends indicate that school choice is growing by about 5% each year with more students choosing charter, private, and homeschooling and this growth was exacerbated by the pandemic. Growing enrollment will continue to be a conversation because it drives funding, which provides stability, which in turn feeds enrollment.

The pandemic made it possible for this type of reform because the district collectively had lost over 300 students to other school choices, and leaders were enthusiastic for ideas that made our system relevant to families. Families who would have never considered choosing an alternative school option are now more aware of the possibilities. As more students possibly experience success and joy in these alternative options, this is leading to a sea change within education. In the end, that is what we want anyways. If a child is best served in an arts program, or a gifted and talented class, or an online school we should all be committed to meeting the needs of that individual student.

COVID-19 does not seem to be breaking anytime soon, and this could lead to a whole new vocabulary around pandemics that were once-in-a-lifetime and now may be more cyclical. District and school leaders should start with a needs assessment of the community to see what they want and what is worrying them. Trends will start to emerge and a critical mass will build to develop and finance new approaches and opportunities to better serve students.

Next Steps for New Code Academy

In building an online school, the district entered into an evolving landscape of school choice and open enrollment. Bloomington Public Schools, which is situated in a major metropolitan area, was already contending with charter, private, and other public schools for both enrollment into and out of the district. The K-12 online market, which previously was led by a small group of charter schools within Minnesota, has been a new educational industry to navigate. The digital learning team discussed what would make NCA stand out amongst other emerging online options and how to communicate the model beyond the district. It was decided that NCA would offer computer science education for students K-12 as it was a current strength of the district. For the elementary school, this included the addition of a computer science specialist that students would see every other week starting in the 2021–2022 school year. The digital learning team worked with CEL Marketing Company to redefine the program's brand and build a marketing strategy to attract families from across the state.

With the speed of development in year one (2020–2021), the focus of year two has been refining pedagogical practices including building independent learners, creating an equitable learning environment, and strengthening the interdisciplinary curriculum. In addition to computer science education, the school funded summer teacher time to reflect and iterate their plans based on their experience in year one. It was their first moment for many to not have to build the plane while flying it. This reflective period resulted in a school-wide conscious discipline behavior matrix, a revamping of the Wednesday schedule, a new attendance policy, the addition of support structures into, and a new family and staff handbook. In partnership with the Learning + Technologies Collaborative and the district's Research, Evaluation, and Assessment Department, NCA instructional leaders will use qualitative and quantitative data to identify problems of practice and opportunities for improvement. NCA's research partnership reduces complacency by keeping a focus on understanding and refinement of online instructional practices and program design.

Spotlight on Practice: Developing Mutually Beneficial Partnerships to Strengthen Your Online Program

Dr. Cassie Scharber, Associate Professor of Learning Technologies and Director of the Learning and Technologies Collaborative, University of Minnesota

Research-Practice Partnerships (RPP) are mutually beneficial, long-term collaborations between practitioners and researchers that address problems of practice. The RPP between Bloomington Public Schools (BPS) and the Learning + Technologies Collaborative (LTC) began in

2019 as a partnership to build equitable computer science pathways and has expanded to also focus on creating a K-12 online school. As the research partner in this collaboration, we develop relationships with district staff to learn more about the district's education and community contexts, share useful research and practical resources to support teaching and learning, and co-facilitate professional learning activities. We also co-develop practice-based research questions with district leaders, collect and analyze data to provide insights to these questions that inform district decision making, and simultaneously contribute to research knowledge in the areas of computer science education and online learning.

An RPP is an effective model that benefits all involved. Researchers benefit from studying teaching and learning in real settings and schools benefit from results from co-created research that is directly relevant to them. These partnerships are regularly funded through grants, foundations, or sponsorships. As schools and districts develop and launch new educational programming related to online learning and more, K-12 leaders should consider ways to bring in outside perspectives and strategize where this expertise would be most beneficial.

As an immediate response to the pandemic and a long-term commitment to provide an online pathway for its students, BPS decided to create a K-12 online school. We collaborated closely with the BPS digital learning team in summer 2020 to build and plan this school through formal work sessions and impromptu problem-solving calls. Our LTC team sifted through research on online learning, Universal Design for Learning, and culturally responsive teaching to create resources and professional learning for teachers on topics like ways to structure time in an online school day/week, effective video length, ideas for asynchronous learning activities, and strategies for building community online. Most of these topics have not been studied in K-12 settings, so we complemented and refined insights from this research to also account for how people learn, the social/emotional/cognitive development of children and adolescents, and the transition to online teaching and learning. In addition to our expertise in online education, we have worked with and in schools for over 20 years and previously worked as K-12 educators ourselves, so we were confident in making these bridges to K-12 education.

Once the school year launched in fall 2020, our roles shifted to providing just-in-time support and collecting/analyzing data that could be used to improve the school. Our perspective and position from outside the district are crucial in the research part of our collaboration because it can be difficult for district leaders to be impartial to teacher, student, and family feedback when it is connected to their professional identity, employment, and energy. As outside partners we can also identify issues or needs that staff within the district may not feel comfortable doing due to internal politics or power dynamics. After analyzing research data, we share the results with district leaders to inform the co-identified problems of practice. This sharing involves conversation between the partners including brainstorms about next steps.

We are excited to continue and grow our partnership with Bloomington Public Schools to both strengthen this program in the district as well as advocate for educational policies, preservice teacher preparation, and perspectives of online students and families across Minnesota.

Next Steps for K-5 Online Learning

In addition to growing and strengthening the program, the digital learning team has become involved in online learning state policy. The rapid growth of online learning within public institutions has illuminated how outdated and dysfunctional policies and oversights are for online learning. Members of the digital learning team have begun advocating and informing policy efforts such as the Minnesota Online Learning Options Act work group to add public education's voice to needed changes. Additionally, the mad dash to create online programs has created competition amongst public institutions as K-12 students are open-enrolling to different districts and bringing funding with them. The Bloomington digital learning team is leading with collaboration by sharing plans and resources with colleagues and at professional development events to counteract this competitive spirit. While there is pride and a sense of ownership in what NCA has developed, public education—online included—must remain united to support the needs of all learners.

Spotlight on Practice: A Music Specialists Reflections on Moving Online

Kelly Yurecko, New Code Academy, K-5 Music Specialist

"How does one turn 25 years of classroom experience into a successful online program?" The question swirled in my mind as I hung up the phone and turned to my husband, second-guessing what I had just done. My son's medical needs had driven me to make the difficult decision to leave my K-5 music room and move everything I thought I knew about teaching music to an online format.

I had about three months to learn as much as I could before the start of the 2020–2021 school year. I studied, listened, watched, planned, spent sleepless nights pouring over every word I might script so my time online was effective, and I threw half of it out the window as I began the process of connecting with kids. It was one of the most humbling, challenging, yet rewarding years of my life. I'm so grateful that I took the risk and moved out of my comfort zone to embrace an entirely new style of teaching online.

If I could go back and give myself some advice, I would have connected more and planned less. I would have checked in with my own two kiddos regarding their level of enjoyment and engagement with my content, rather than justifying my choices to them. Above all, I would have given myself a bit more grace when it came to transitioning an "in-person" discipline to something entirely remote. Here's what I would have said to that tentative individual embarking on a new road:

1. **Embrace technology.** When it wasn't possible to connect with a technology specialist, Google and YouTube became my best friends. There were times that I needed information on how to use a tool or website ASAP. Those moments became strangely empowering, as I realized that I could pull from my own knowledge bank and resources to get the job done.
2. **Learn and grow from your data analysis.** Sitting in a classroom with twenty other students, I wasn't always aware as a classroom teacher what these "individuals" before me were capable of. The data I was getting from individual students online made it glaringly obvious where my shortcomings were as a teacher. I adjusted to ensure understanding and committed to this ongoing process of evolution for all.
3. **Believe in yourself.** Despite my best efforts and intentions, I was unable to satisfy every parent that came across my program. Never had I been so visible to parents, and everything from my choice of attire to my curriculum offerings was being criticized as I entered their homes for daily instruction. Initially, I succumbed to bouts of anxiety as I hyper-analyzed my instruction, interactions with students, and intended outcomes. Through having some honest, sometimes difficult conversations with parents, we found common ground to stand on as we moved forward into better experiences for all.
4. **Get ready to pivot.** My aspirations of becoming the world's greatest online music teacher shifted quickly as I realized I was planning way too much. Students having difficulty walking cannot be expected to perform jump rope maneuvers correctly. Online learning requires a specific set of skills that must be built upon in order to succeed. In slowing down instruction and monitoring my kiddos for understanding, I found that we had much more consistent success once our skills foundation was established.

5. **Celebrate and collaborate.** Critics of online learning argue that it is challenging to make connections with students and families using this medium. I respectfully disagree; my role as collaborator became even more important to me as I saw glimpses into the everyday lives of my students—ups, downs, challenges, family dynamics—and I developed very rewarding relationships as we worked together to achieve common goals of success and growth.

If you are pondering making the leap into the world of online education, commit to ongoing learning. Strike that delicate balance between work and personal obligations and focus on developing relationships first. Go slow initially to make more curriculum gains, and don't sweat the small stuff. You are providing an invaluable service that works well for students and families, and your efforts are not wasted. You are seen, respected, and valued!

Just as NCA teachers needed to immerse themselves in the online environment to truly learn how to become online teachers and adjust their pedagogical approaches; NCA instructional leaders grew from the tidal wave of problem solving required to develop new learning within an old system. It is not often that an opportunity comes along to create a new school with the potential to engage learners who experienced failure in traditional education; as well as provide families with the flexibility of geographic location and the security of a physically safe learning environment. The field of elementary online education is evolving rapidly and with it comes the chance for educators to grow professionally. Hopefully this book served as a resource in that evolution.

Reference

Collins, J. (2001). *Good to great: Why some companies make the leap and others don't*. HarperBusiness.

Glossary

Asynchronous Learning: Any learning, practice, or assessment that takes place outside of a live virtual Google Meet.

Bloomington Online School: The name of the school during the 2020–2021 school year.

Breakout Rooms: A feature of Google Meet that allows the facilitator to break students into any variety of small groups. Additional features include a time limit on the small group, the ability for the teacher to pre-schedule groups and move between small groups, and the ability for students to request help from the teacher while in their small group.

Brick-and-Mortar: A term used to describe a physical building or facility where students go to learn.

Culminating Assessments: End-of-unit assessments that are designed as performance tasks that provide student voice, choice, and ownership of learning. Culminating assessments correlate directly with the essential questions of the unit and allow students to creatively demonstrate their understanding of the essential questions.

Digital Competency: A component of NCA's first 20 days' curriculum that focuses on teaching students the cognitive and technical skills needed to navigate learning online. Examples include navigating Seesaw, utilizing Google Meet, and submitting assignments online.

Emergency Remote Teaching: A temporary learning model that was put in place in the spring of 2020 to accommodate at home learning due to the world-wide pandemic.

Fluid Practice: The use of different instructional strategies and adoption of new beliefs as teachers transition from brick and mortar to online teaching.

Independent Learning Assignments: Assignments that teachers create on Seesaw for students to complete asynchronously that provide an opportunity for students to demonstrate their understanding of standards and benchmarks.

Interdisciplinary Curriculum: Curriculum that integrates multiple subject areas standards and benchmarks into one unit, lesson, activity, assessment, etc.

Learning Coach: An adult that is present during online learning that students access for support, encouragement, and guidance. At NCA, we encourage learning coaches to take on the support roles of communication with teacher and school, building routines, encouraging screen-free breaks, supporting organization of materials, motivation, and frequent student check-ins.

Live Instruction: Any instruction that takes place in a whole group or small group setting on a live Google Meet.

New Code Academy: The rebranded name of our school during the 2021–2022 school year that signifies the addition of computer science instruction and pedagogy.

Social Justice: The practice of allyship and coalition work in order to promote equality, equity, respect, and the assurance of rights within and between communities and social groups.

Station Rotation Model: A learning model that involves students rotating from one learning station to the next wherein at least one station requires a digital learning component. For example, students might rotate between digital IXL math practice, to a partner math game, to an instructional small group with the teacher.

Synchronous Learning: Any learning that is done as a whole group or small group in a live Google Meet.

Appendix

First 20 Days of School Planning Template

TABLE A.1 Steps One Through Four in Planning the First 20 Days

Planning the First 20 Days
Step 1: While thinking towards the end-goal established in the pre-thinking activity, brainstorm the tech competencies, community and relationship building skills, and rituals and routines the teacher should address for the week.
Step 2: Prioritize and sequence those ideas across the week.
Step 3: Plan the specifics for each day with the goal of students achieving those competencies and skills each day within the framework of the daily schedule.
Step 4: Scan for horizontal and vertical alignment. Does each day logically flow into the next? Does each week build on the previous week? Are scaffolds in place to support all learners?

TABLE A.2 Weekly Overview Template for the First 20 Days

Weekly overview of skills introduced		
Tech Competencies	Community and Relationship Building	Rituals & Routines
• What tools do we need to know how to use? • What skills do we need to be able to use those tools?	• Who is in our class? • How are we connected? • How will we get to know one another? • How will we build connections and relationships online? • Where can we provide opportunities for families to get involved?	• What does our day look like? • What expectations are there for teacher and student? • Where can we build opportunities for students to give feedback? • What are our block, morning meeting, & end-of-day routines?

TABLE A.3 Daily Overview Template for the First 20 Days

Daily overview of skills introduced			
	Tech Competencies	Community and Relationship Building	Rituals & Routines
Monday (Day X)			
Tuesday (Day X)			
Wednesday (Day X)			
Thursday (Day X)			
Friday (Day X)			

TABLE A.4 Daily Lesson Plan Template for the First 20 Days

Day of Week (Day X)	Morning Meeting (30 mins) Whole group/ small group	Block 1 (2 hrs) Stations (whole group, small group, independent)	Block 2 (1 hour) Stations (whole group, small group, independent)	End of Day/ Student Check-Ins (50 mins) Whole group/ independent
Standards *if applicable				
Lessons/ Activities Ignite, Chunk, Chew, Review Movement Break Student Voice and Choice Differentiation Digital and Non-Digital				
Formative Assessments and/ or Accountability Tasks				
Supports and Scaffolds Vocabulary Required Background Knowledge Graphic Orgs, etc.				
Materials Needed or Platforms Being Used				

Educator Reflection:
- Whose perspective/voice is represented in these lessons/activities? Whose is missing?
- How can students bring their values/strengths into these lessons/activities?
- Are these lessons/activities inclusive of different kinds of success?
- Can all students access/understand the directions/activity/information/resource?
- What stereotypes might be introduced or reinforced by the use of these resources/activities/content?

To see additional templates, activities, and presentations visit: elementaryonlinelearning.com

Index

accessibility 22–23, 136–137
achievement 25–26
assessment 15, 45–47, 117–118, 139, 187
asynchronous/independent learning: accessibility 136–137; assignments 25; feedback 137–140; independent work 131–132; lesson creation 133–134; and time 140–141; tools 125–126

Bellinger, Kristin 44–45, 119–120
Berry-Blasingame, Janelle 64–65
brain-based learning 55–58
breakout rooms 90, 114–115
brick-and-mortar schools 2, 87–88, 91
Brower, Rebecca 150–152

cameras 121–122
Cannon, Ray 67–68
charter schools 21
classroom management 32, 47, 111–112
Cognitive Load Theory 12–13
Cogswell, Lisa 126–129
collegial presence 11–12, 92
Collins, Jim 178
communication 61–62, 149–152
communities: building 57, 99, 103–105, 168–170; daily meetings 159–163; importance of 157–158; school-wide 163–168
Community of Inquiry 10–12, 158
culturally responsive teaching 15–16
curriculum: accessing 91; building 35–39, 46–47; interdisciplinary 40–44, 48–51, 57

digital competencies 96, 98; *see also* technology
digital resources 6
Drake, Susan 40

emergency remote teaching (ERT) 1–2, 9–10, 21–22, 143–144
engagement 88
English language learners 6, 67, 69, 136
equity 21, 22, 69
example unit outlines 30–31

families 155–156, 178–179
feedback 53–55, 92, 102, 137–140
Fett, Kristen 110–111
Figueroa, R. 12
first 20 days 95–98, 102–103, 105–108
flexibility 15
Floyd, George 9
food 74–75

Gomes, Elizabeth 145–147
Good to Great (Collins) 178
Gunkel, Colleen 23–25, 48–49
Gutiérrez, Rochelle 22, 26–27

Hammond, Zaretta 13, 56
Hollie, Sharocky 23–24
hybrid programs 6

identity 26–27
independent learning *see* asynchronous/independent learning
Individual Education Plans (IEPs) 54
instructional coaching *see* professional development
instructional frameworks 10, 46, 69, 97

Kalkman, Allie 99–100, 171–173
kindergarten 99–102, 110–111

leadership 68–69, 91–92
learning coaches 12, 88–89, 143–147
learning management systems: and communication 152; and curriculum 35; funding 6; and language 23; Seesaw 73, 125; and time 87–88
Lee, M. 12
lesson design: and asynchronous learning 133–134; and content blocks 129; and curriculum 44; and learning management systems 73
live/synchronous learning: active 112–113; cameras 121–122; differentiated 117–119; multimodal 116; online 110; participatory 113; personal 116–117
Loftus, Sara 83–85, 114–115
Lokey-Vega, A. 11

Marohn, Matt 162–163
materials 70–73
Mersch, Rachel 8–9, 71–73
Mezera, Katrina 3–5
movement: breaks 57, 61; and engagement 111, 116; and live instruction 122; and online PE 64–65
multimodal learning 116, 128
Murray, Ruth 106–108

New Code Academy: conception of 5–7; development of 3–5; next steps 179–180
Nienaltowski, Tori 89–90

Office of Educational Equity 23
online learning: adjusting to 78–79, 183–185; building programs 175–177; development of 2–3; next steps 182–183; pre-pandemic 21–22
orientation 147–149

partner schools 66, 69
physical education 64–65
Plaman, Jeff 14–15
play 171–173
power 30
professional development: and online teaching 79–81; problem solving 82–83, 92; reflection 86–87; and social justice 28–29; support 85–86
program design 53–55, 92
program models: and independent learning 139; at NCA 55, 152, 173; and needs of children 74–75; and technology 148

racial injustice 9–10
Reams, Megan 153–155
reform 177–179
relationships 15
relevancy: of assessments 46; of curriculum 45, 48, 50, 163; to families 178–179; to schools 181
Research-Practice Partnerships (RPP) 180–182
rituals and routines 89, 98–99, 129–131

Sanders, K. 11
Scharber, Cassie, Dr. 180–182
schedules 58–61
Schroeder, Gina 78–79
Skadsem, Holly 36
small group instruction 58, 126
social learning 122
special education: delivery of 54, 106–107; need for 6; staffing 67, 69; teams 37
specialists: access to 62–63, 146, 177; and online instruction 183–185; staffing 66–67
staffing 49–50, 63–67, 77–78
structure 15, 58
synchronous learning *see* live/synchronous learning

teacher moves 170–171
technology 73–74, 99–100; *see also* digital competencies
time management 87–88, 140–141

Universal Design for Learning (UDL) 16

Vlasin, Emilee 28–29, 103–105, 139–140
volunteering 153–155

Wahlquist, Emily 134–136
Weber, Anna 168–170
Weisser, John 177–179

Young, Kerry 38–39
Yurecko, Kelly 183–185

For Product Safety Concerns and Information please contact our EU
representative GPSR@taylorandfrancis.com
Taylor & Francis Verlag GmbH, Kaufingerstraße 24, 80331 München, Germany

www.ingramcontent.com/pod-product-compliance
Lightning Source LLC
Chambersburg PA
CBHW062227300426
44115CB00012BA/2255